# POLITICS AND ECONOMICS

# POLITICS
# AND ECONOMICS

*Papers in Political Economy*

BY

LORD ROBBINS

LONDON
MACMILLAN & CO LTD
NEW YORK · ST MARTIN'S PRESS
1963

MACMILLAN AND COMPANY LIMITED
*St Martin's Street London WC2*
*also Bombay Calcutta Madras Melbourne*

THE MACMILLAN COMPANY OF CANADA LIMITED
*Toronto*

ST MARTIN'S PRESS INC
*New York*

PRINTED IN GREAT BRITAIN

TO MY FRIENDS
AT THE LONDON SCHOOL
OF ECONOMICS

# PREFACE

THE papers in this collection fall into three divisions.

The first consists of a single paper, 'On the Relations between Politics and Economics', in which an attempt is made to assess the influence on politics of economic thought and the extent to which any theory of economic policy is itself dependent on political assumptions. These are matters on which I have written a certain amount in the past, but, since I have never succeeded in making my views immune from misunderstanding, I hope that this more systematic treatment will not be thought to be superfluous.

The second division comprises six papers which, in various ways, are concerned with the general theory of the state and relations between states, with special reference to the principles of economic policy. The first, 'Freedom and Order', is in the nature of a confession of faith on ultimate ends and means. The two following, 'Art and the State' and 'Equality as a Social Objective', consist of elucidations and applications of some of the points raised therein, while the fourth, 'Hayek on Liberty', a review article on Professor Hayek's thought-provoking and courageous *Constitution of Liberty*, affords the opportunity for further discussion of ultimate conceptions and their history. The last two papers in this division, 'The Meaning of Economic Integration' and 'Liberalism and the International Problem', are concerned with international relations, both from an economic and a more general point of view.

The third division consists of three papers of a rather more technical nature, concerned with problems of high finance. The first, a review article on Sir Donald Mac-Dougall's important book on the Dollar Problem, develops a little, with special reference to Sir Donald's analysis and predictions, a point of view which I have elaborated at some length in the central papers of my *Economist in the Twentieth*

*Century,* and expresses a scepticism with regard to dollar shortage which I should like to keep on the record. The second ,'Thoughts on the Crisis of 1957' is a series of reflections on the financial difficulties of 1957 and the measures adopted to deal with them. It owed its origin, I confess, to gross misrepresentation in the Press and elsewhere of what I was alleged to have done and said in this connection; and, in this aspect, no doubt, it has a very fugitive value. But, as it contains extensive applications and illustrations of general principles to which I continue to attach considerable importance, I think that it is still worth preserving. The final paper is a discussion of certain aspects of the *Radcliffe Report on the Working of the Monetary System.*

None of these papers was written with a view to publication on a unified plan. As will be seen from the footnotes, they consist chiefly of lectures written for special audiences or essays prompted by reflections on particular problems or books; and in collecting them for publication, while I have not hesitated to revise or to expand where it seemed desirable, I have made no attempt to eliminate the expository modes which their various origins involved. Nevertheless, I venture to hope that, as they are now presented, they may yet reveal sufficient of a coherent outlook to warrant republication in this form.

I have inscribed this book to those governors and teachers of the London School of Economics who, when the Senate of the University of London had refused to sanction the tenure of my Chair on a part-time basis, rallied to my support with generous practical action, making still possible, in the institution in which I have served so happily for so many years, the continued pursuit of those academic interests and activities which have been the main inspiration of my working life.

ROBBINS

THE LONDON SCHOOL OF ECONOMICS
*August* 1961

# CONTENTS

# PART I

# 1

## ON THE RELATIONS BETWEEN
## POLITICS AND ECONOMICS [1]

### I

THE subject of my lecture is the relations between economics and politics. I was led to this theme by reflection
on the contrast between two statements on this subject by
Cournot and Keynes; and perhaps I can best begin by
quoting these two masters.

At the end of his *Recherches sur les principes mathématiques
de la théorie des richesses* Cournot says:

> . . . it must be recognized that such questions as that of
> commercial liberty are not settled either by the arguments of
> scientific men or even by the wisdom of statesmen. A higher
> power drives nations in this direction or that, and when the
> day of a system is past, good reasons cannot restore its lost
> vitality any more than sophisms. The skill of statesmen, then,
> consists in tempering the ardour of the spirit of innovation,
> without attempting an impossible struggle against the laws of
> Providence. Possession of a sound theory may help in this
> labour of resistance to abrupt changes and assist in easing the
> transition from one system to another. By giving more light
> on a debated point, it soothes the passions which are aroused.
> Systems have their fanatics, but the science which succeeds to
> systems never has them. Finally, even if theories relating to
> social organization do not guide the doings of the day, they
> at least throw light on the history of accomplished facts. Up
> to a certain point it is possible to compare the influence of
> economic theories on society to that of grammarians on
> language. Languages are formed without the consent of
> grammarians, and are corrupted in spite of them; but their
> works throw light on the laws of the formation and decadence

[1] This is the English text of a lecture delivered at the Collège de France
on May 29th, 1961, under the Chairmanship of Professor François Perroux.

3

of languages; and their rules hasten the time when a language attains its perfection, and delay a little the invasions of barbarism and bad taste which corrupt it.[1]

The statement by Keynes also comes as a peroration. In the last paragraph of the *General Theory* he says:

> the ideas of economists and political philosophers, both when they are right and when they are wrong, are more powerful than is commonly understood. Indeed the world is ruled by little else. Practical men, who believe themselves to be quite exempt from any intellectual influences, are usually the slaves of some defunct economist. Madmen in authority, who hear voices in the air, are distilling their frenzy from some academic scribbler of a few years back. I am sure that the power of vested interests is vastly exaggerated compared with the gradual encroachment of ideas. Not, indeed, immediately, but after a certain interval; for in the field of economic and political philosophy there are not many who are influenced by new theories after they are twenty-five or thirty years of age, so that the ideas which civil servants and politicians and even agitators apply to current events are not likely to be the newest. But, soon or late, it is ideas, not vested interests, which are dangerous for good or evil.[2]

There is thus a very sharp contrast between the statements of these two very great economists. Yet those of us who are economists all probably have moods in which each carries persuasion: sometimes we think that we can do very little, sometimes we have much more confidence. It occurred to me, therefore, when I received your kind invitation, that perhaps some good purpose might be served by further reflection on the subject. My lecture will fall into four main parts: I shall enquire first how in fact economists have conceived their rôle in relation to the business of government; I shall then, secondly, discuss the actual influence on politics of certain leading economic ideas; thirdly, I shall examine in some detail the way in which some economists have attempted to elaborate economic norms of political

[1] *Op. cit.* (Bacon's translation, New York 1927, p. 171. The original passage is on pp. 197-8 of Lutfalla's edition).
[2] *Op. cit.* pp. 383-4.

4

action: and, finally, I shall come back to the fundamental question posed by my quotations and ask what are legitimate expectations in this respect.

## II

To begin, then, with historical notions.

There can be no doubt that throughout history economists of all schools have conceived their work as having the most intimate bearing on politics, both in the sense of the theory of political action and of the actual practice of affairs.

Thus, we know that, in the beginning, much of what has now become technical analysis, takes its rise from the pamphlets of merchants and court officials anxious to promote or to resist particular acts of policy. And even the broader generalizations regarding the nature of economic society, which we find in the works of Plato and Aristotle and philosophers of the Scholastic tradition, occurred in contexts intimately concerned with conceptions of political obligation. Both the theory of money and the theory of the division of labour originated in what are essentially *political* discussions.

This attitude and this conjunction persist long after a synthesis of scientific generalization, much more comprehensive than these incidental pronouncements, has begun to make its appearance. Both in the literature of Physiocracy and in the works of the great eighteenth-century Scotch moralists the mixture of political prescription with economic analysis is so close as often to present great difficulties of disentanglement: Quesnay and Mercier de la Rivière present their economic generalizations as part of an exposition of natural law and order. Adam Smith describes political economy as 'a branch of the science of a statesman' and ascribes to it in that rôle two distinct objects: 'first, to provide a plentiful revenue or subsistence for the people, or, more properly, to enable them to provide such a revenue or subsistence for themselves; and, secondly, to supply the state or commonwealth with a revenue sufficient for the public services'. 'It proposes', he says, 'to enrich both

5

the people and the sovereign.'[1]  Indeed, so much are political norms and economic descriptions intertwined in the works of the eighteenth-century writers, that great confusion has arisen among later commentators : it has been thought that their economic analysis stood or fell with the acceptability of their political philosophy — which, of course, is not at all true.  The validity of the Physiocratic theory of circulation or Adam Smith's analysis of value and distribution was quite independent of the solution to the question whether the processes they described led to good or bad results.

As time goes on a greater degree of sophistication becomes more general.  Ricardo was certainly aware that certain fundamental decisions lay outside his competence as an economist.  'We cannot be quite sure', he says, 'that provided he is equally well fed, a man may not be happier in the enjoyment of the luxury of idleness than in the enjoyment of the luxuries of a neat cottage and good clothes.'[2]  By the middle of the nineteenth century the distinction between Political Economy as an art and Political Economy as a science, discussed at length by Nassau Senior in his Oxford Lectures of 1852,[3] had become generally recognized.  Later on, particularly in the work of Henry Sidgwick and the elder Keynes,[4] this becomes subsumed under the broader distinction between normative and positive propositions in social studies generally.  In our own day the minute search for implicit value judgments, which perhaps begins with the systematic study of the index number problem, has even become something of a heresy hunt — and, like most heresy hunts, something of a bore.  Woe betide the wretched economist who, discussing the implications of measures likely to create one hundred per cent unemployment, does not add the warning 'whether this is a good thing or a bad thing involves, of course, a judgment of value !'

But with all this, I do not doubt that the focus of economics on politics, at least in the more abstract sense, has

---

[1] Wealth of Nations, Cannan's edition, vol. i, p. 395.
[2] Works, Ed. Sraffa, vol. vii, p. 185.          [3] Op. cit. pp. 36-56.
[4] See his Scope and Method of Political Economy, chapter II, passim.

remained very intimate. Economists may have come to realize — very rightly, in my judgment — that *as economists* they have nothing to say on the true ends of life : and that their propositions concerning what *is* or what *can be* involve in themselves no propositions concerning what *ought to be*. They may have come to insist on the neutrality of their generalizations — a protective measure, both against those who accuse them of secret bias and against those who would illicitly involve them in distasteful propaganda. But few become economists from mere curiosity ; considered as pure knowledge, our subject, although not without its Faustian moments, has far less attraction than many others. And although, as life goes on, a man becomes habituated to what he is doing and no longer asks himself so frequently as he did when he was young what is its further purpose, yet few, I fancy, of those whom we would regard as worth while, are not sustained in their general attitude by the belief that somehow or other what they are doing is useful and may contribute to the common weal. There are those who have said otherwise — the classic observation of Cantillon on the population question is a case in point,[1] and we have had the Olympian pretensions of the later Pareto. But there is the irony of the Enlightenment in Cantillon ; and Pareto's somewhat shrill insistences were an obvious, and in the end a somewhat fatiguing, pose. In my submission, it is clear that the majority of economists aspire to some influence on politics, both as a system of thought and in manifestations of practical action.

To what extent have such aspirations been successful ? This brings me to the second division of my enquiry.

### III

If we date the rise of systematic economics from the circulation of Cantillon's manuscript or the publication of

---

[1] 'It is also a question outside of my subject whether it is better to have a great multitude of inhabitants, poor and badly provided, than a smaller number, much more at their ease : a million who consume the produce of 6 acres or 4 millions who live on the produce of an acre and a half.' *Essai sur la nature du commerce*, Higgs' edition, p. 85.

Hume's Essays, I do not think it can be denied that in one way or another there has been a very considerable influence of economic thought on practice. Let us look at a few conspicuous examples.

I take first the rise of liberalism — the breaking-down of statutory monopolies, the pressure for the liberation of trade and migration, the campaign against arbitrary privilege. Now I should be sorry to oversimplify the origins of this great movement: I would not wish to underestimate the influence either of material conditions or of the pure passion for personal liberty. He would be blind who would ignore the changes in economic conditions which gave rise to the growing ascendancy of *bourgeois* wealth and the power of commercial and industrial urban populations resentful of feudal privilege; and he would be unwise who denied — as some have denied — the influence of pure political idealism, the love of liberty in itself, and the hatred of arbitrary power. Who but a fool would attribute to *bourgeois* interest the passion of a Tocqueville or a J. S. Mill?

Nevertheless, there was much more involved than the brute force of material interest and the dogmatic affirmation of political ideals. So far as the economic side of the movement was concerned, there was a formidable background of intellectual analysis. And indeed it is difficult to believe that it could have been otherwise. For, however much you may believe in liberty for its own sake, you are unlikely, unless you are mentally unbalanced, to recommend liberty if there is reason to believe that liberty must necessarily involve chaos. Therefore, before the leaders of eighteenth- and nineteenth-century liberalism could recommend liberty in economic relations, it was necessary that there should exist a body of thought which showed, or which purported to show, that, if left uncontrolled save by due process of law, individual initiative in the economic sphere would not lead to economic disaster: that is to say, it was necessary to show that the interplay of spontaneous self-interest would harmonize with public good.

As we know, it was just such an analysis which was

8

provided by contemporary economists. Both Quesnay and his followers in France and Hume and Adam Smith in Great Britain, unfolded a view of economic life which seemed to show, beneath the complex of arbitrary regulation, a system of spontaneous relations which, if left to itself within an appropriate framework of law and order, might be expected to function harmoniously. And, whatever the deficiencies of this analysis as revealed by subsequent thought and experiment, it yet possessed sufficient intellectual coherence and persuasive power to exercise a most powerful influence on policy. Any account, for instance, of the coming of free trade in the United Kingdom which omitted the influence of economic thought and of economists would be defective and, indeed, absurd. And, apart from spectacular episodes of this sort, in hundreds of subtler ways, Western policy and Western institutions have been influenced by this ideology.

I take as my second example an exactly contrasting tendency, the rise of Marxian communism, an historical development of which, in our day, it would be difficult to deny the importance.

Here again I should be sorry to be thought to be claiming any absolute pre-eminence for the influence of economic thought. It is true that the history of events in Russia falsifies to an overwhelming degree the expectations of Marxian analysis that the revolution would come first in the centres of advanced capitalism; it indeed is a standing example of the extent to which a group of determined, and well-organized men, inspired by cut and dried ideas, can change the course of history contrary to expectations. But I should hesitate to describe the Messianic element in Marxian thought, the element which gives it perhaps its main appeal and dynamic force, as economic in character. It springs rather from the deep unconscious unhappiness of the human race, its sense of injustice on the earth and the feeling, which we all have had — at least in our weaker moments — that if only one sufficiently violent convulsive effort be made, destructive of all that apparatus of daily life which seems to hem us in

9

and frustrate us, all will suddenly be well. The ancestors of Marx on this plane are not the economists attempting rationally to analyse and understand the world, but rather the ancient prophets with their denunciation of sin and wrongdoing and their blinding vision of sudden deliverance. The terrific peroration of the chapter in *Das Capital* on the Historical Tendency of Accumulation, with its obvious Freudian symbolism, in which the 'integument' of capitalism is 'burst asunder' and 'the expropriators are expropriated'[1] is reminiscent, not of Quesnay and Ricardo, but of Amos and Isaiah.

Nevertheless, the form in which all this was made manifest — the shop-window of logical argument — was deeply influenced by economic analysis. It is true that, so far as the vision of the future was concerned, there was very little of all this. It is one of the curiosities of the history of thought that so little attention was paid by Marx and his followers to the principles of economic planning : any attempt to forecast the machinery of that state which was to come to birth when the integument of capitalism burst asunder, was under a ban — it was 'unscientific' curiosity. But the *description* of contemporary *institutions*, the diagnosis of exploitation with its increasing poverty and instability, were all cast in the form of severe, even pretentious, economic analysis : certainly, we get the perspective of history awry if, whether we think him right or wrong, we are not prepared to recognize Marx as one of the most formidable of the Ricardian economists. It is safe to say that if there had been no labour theory of value, no subsistence theory of wages, no exploitation theory of interest, the whole Marxian movement must have had an entirely different language ; and the sense of *scientific* inevitability of the argument which, ill-founded though it may be, has influenced so many powerful intellects, would have been absent. And if anyone suggests that all that has had no influence on history, one can only say to him, look around !

Finally, since one of my opening texts is a question from

[1] *Op. cit.* Kerr's edition, p. 837.

the *General Theory*, I will take the influence of the thought of Keynes himself. There can be no doubt of what he himself believed : he had supreme confidence that, once there had been time for his new ideas to be assimilated, they would exercise a powerful and perhaps a decisive effect on policy.

In the event this confidence has proved to be fully justified. Indeed, the rapidity with which the Keynesian approach has become part and parcel of the legislative and administrative practice of the free world must be something unique in history. The belief that it is the duty of states, through their budget and through the control of money to maintain an appropriate stability of aggregate demand, has become so firmly established in our system of thought that it often seems difficult to do justice to the state of mind of those who, according to their lights, attempted to carry on without it. It is not true that we are all Keynesians now. But most of us are — after our fashion.

The whole episode of the reception of these views is a very apt illustration of the way in which thought may influence action. It would be quite wrong to regard the characteristic Keynesian prescriptions as fundamentally new. Quite apart from the heretic fringe from Malthus onwards (who, however, had usually got the logic of the argument quite wrong), there was a long and honourable ancestry of more orthodox thinkers who had emphasized the essential instability of the monetary equilibrium and who had urged upon the state remedial measures which were similar in kind, if not in degree, to those put forward by Keynes himself. It needed the background of the Great Depression and the sense of the insufficiency of traditional liberal financial policy which that entailed, to create an intellectual atmosphere in which arguments of this sort were likely to be heard with attention by practical men. Nevertheless, it would be a crude error to regard the arguments themselves or their effect on the course of history as a mere by-product, an epiphenomenon, of economic history. Public receptivity may indeed have been due to the depression. But what was received was economic thought of a specific character ; and although there were elements in that thought which were a response to the circumstances of the depression, there was much more in it than that. It does not need much imagination to conceive alternative doctrines which might easily have suited the public mood : indeed, we know that there was strong competition on the Left. As it was, it was these ideas, argued with unsurpassable eloquence and expository skill, which gained the day ; and in the light of history they may well be thought to have changed the prospects of survival of the free society.

IV

And so I could go on. But I think, perhaps, that these three examples may be regarded as sufficient evidence for the view, represented by my quotation from Keynes, that economic ideas can play, and have played, an important rôle in history.

The question therefore arises — and this leads to the third division of my enquiry — whether it is not possible to construct, on the basis of economic theory alone, some system of rules and prescriptions which may be hoped to exert a continuous influence on politics and which may be regarded as having, so to speak, a logical right to do so. And there can be little doubt that a vision of this sort has hovered before the eyes of successive generations of economists, especially, perhaps, those of the English-speaking tradition. Not a system which should completely supersede politics — it was always recognized that there were problems of defence and criminal law, which involved considerations lying outside economics — but a system so unequivocal in its prescriptions regarding the conduct of what was conceived as *economic* policy that, within this sphere, its logic, if not its power to coerce unreasoning politicians, might be regarded as all-compelling. This vision has alternative forms which I should like to examine briefly.

To begin with the English classical economists. Now it is quite true that these thinkers were pre-eminently concerned with policy, to a much greater degree indeed than any of their modern successors. It is also quite true that we find in their writings that more or less clear-cut distinction between the pursuit of wealth and of other objectives which may seem to make plausible the idea of a more or less separate body of prescriptions regarding the former; and there are certainly hints of such a separation to be found from time to time.[1]

Nevertheless, I should be inclined to argue that there was much less of this in their actual practice or indeed in their underlying assumptions than with writers who came later. The classical theory of economic policy was in fact shot through with recognition of political objectives and values. This is very obvious, in its pronouncements on any detailed problem — the relief of poverty, for instance, or popular education. It is little less obvious in their more general treatment of the subject. The test of utility was acknowledged by them all, not only Bentham and his followers, but by all the other leading figures from Hume onwards:[2] and this was quite clearly a *political* criterion equally applicable to all types of action — defence and opulence might be contrasted, but each was subordinate to the greatest happiness principle. And we have Bentham's own confession that he could not conceive of a code of laws concerning political economy distinct and separate from all other codes. 'The collection of laws upon this subject would only be a mass of imperfect shreds drawn without distinction from the whole body of laws.'[3] I would not claim that the classical economists had clearly perceived the misleading nature of any definition which limits the applicability of

[1] As, for example, in Senior's *Lectures* referred to above and also in J. S. Mill's early paper on definitions in the *Unsettled Questions of Political Economy*. But as regards Mill it is worthy of note that the title of his main work was *Principles of Political Economy with some of their Applications to Social Philosophy*, and that in the discussion of practical questions here the appeal is almost continuous to assumptions of a *political* nature.

[2] See the illuminating account of a conversation between Senior and de Broglie in the former's *Conversations with M. Thiers, M. Guizot and other Distinguished Persons*, ii, p. 176.

[3] See the *View of a Complete Code of Laws, Works*, Ed. Bowring, vol. iii, p. 203.

economic considerations to anything less than the whole
sphere of rational action. But I do not think it is open to
question that their theory of economic policy was essentially
*political* economy and depended for its applicability upon the
acknowledgment of overriding political values.

At first sight there seems much less of this in more recent
developments. The so-called welfare economics, at least
before it lost self-confidence, unquestionably owed much to
the traditions of classical analysis. But the look of the thing
was different and, on the surface at least, the degree of
dependence on political norms. It is not denied for a
moment that there may be considerations, other than those
relating to the national dividend and its distribution, which
may be relevant to policy: in some respects, perhaps,
writers of this school may be thought to be more sensitive
to 'non-economic' values than some of their classical predecessors. But the suggestion was certainly present that
here is a body of rules concerning the relation between welfare and the production and distribution of wealth which is
*independent* of political valuations, and that although from
time to time, political valuations may override these rules, yet
there is a fair presumption that they provide, as it were, *non-
political* indications of appropriate policy.

Now I should be very sorry to be thought to underrate
the value of some of the work which has been done in this
field. Its classic manifestation, Pigou's great *Economics of
Welfare*, is obviously one of the more notable intellectual
achievements, in our sphere, of the first half of this century;
and, properly interpreted, it contains much which is important and relevant to practice. But any claim that its generalizations and norms of measurement are independent of
politics is surely based on illusion. For, in the last analysis,
any assertions about the movement of welfare as a whole
must depend upon assumptions regarding the compara-
bility of one person's welfare with another's; and these, in
the nature of things, are matters of political philosophy —
conventions imported from outside. I would not deny that
with the aid of conventions of this sort it may be possible to

derive conclusions of great power and significance : all that I contend is that these conventions must be regarded as *extra-economic* in origin, and therefore that the alleged neutrality of a system based, for instance, on the egalitarian norm is just as open to question in that respect as that of a system based upon norms of any other character.

In this connection, I suggest the practitioners of this kind of welfare economics do much less justice to the facts of the case than did their predecessors. For, contrary to popular belief, Bentham at least was completely conscious of the essentially conventional nature of the famous calculus of pleasure and pain. ''Tis in vain', he said, 'to talk of adding quantities which after the addition will continue distinct as before, one man's happiness will never be another man's happiness . . . you might as well pretend to add twenty apples to twenty pears. . . . This addibility of the happiness of different subjects, . . . however . . . fictitious . . . is a *postulatum* [my italics] without the allowance of which all practical reasoning is at a stand.' [1] Whether, in fact, practical reasoning does come to a stand, if actual adding operations are suspended, is perhaps an open question. But, I submit that the conventional nature thereof is something which has only to be clearly stated for recognition to be inescapable.

There is a further variant of classical thought which deserves examination in this connection. Starting from the *desideratum* of the maximum freedom rather than maximum utility, there is a certain school of liberal thought which seeks to derive, *via* economic analysis, the structure of what may be called a voluntaristic society. It is clear from what I have just said that there is no question here of independence of ultimate political values. But the extent to which, given the original objective, the rest can be conceived to follow without the further intrusion of politics is a matter which repays further attention.

The type of thought which I have in mind starts from

---

[1] Quoted from a manuscript in the University College collection by Halévy in his *Growth of Philosophical Radicalism*, p. 495.

the analysis of the market. As is well known, given the supply of goods, the operation of the market can be represented as a process of rationing by the purse : the available stocks are allotted to those who are prepared to pay most for them. At the same time, given the supplies of productive agents and the disposition of their owners to work and to invest, it can be represented as a process of continuous control of the organization of production. If at any point there is an abnormal gap — positive or negative — between prices and costs, that is an indication that more could be produced in price terms by a re-allocation of productive services towards or away from that area. A productive system worked in this way may, therefore, be conceived as a process of response to a continuous general election on the principle of proportionate representation. The entrepreneur may, so to speak, put up the candidates ; he may attempt to sway the election by propaganda and persuasion ; but the ultimate decision lies with those who spend — with what is sometimes called the sovereignty of the consumer.[1] And since this is thought to represent the maximum of liberty conceivable in this respect for the individual citizens, it follows without more ado that the objective of policy should be to remove as far as possible all obstacles to its realization — monopolistic restriction, discriminatory commodity taxation, the ignorance of market forces on the part of consumer and producer, and so on.

The conception is a splendid one and it has not been without its admirers in the collectivist, as well as in the liberal, camp. But even if, for the time being, we neglect the whole question of the initial distribution of power to demand and supply, it should be clear that it leaves out of the picture the control of large and essential areas of pro-

---

[1] This term is not perhaps an altogether happy one. For, of course, as the above formulation implies, it is not only the preferences of the citizens as consumers, but also their preferences as workers and investors, which must be conceived as determining the total situation. But the general conception is clear enough. For a forceful and illuminating presentation of this point of view, see W. H. Hutt, *Economists and the Public*, a work whose merits of candour, erudition, and argumentative force have not yet received sufficient recognition.

ductive activity. We can, if we are so minded, conceive of a market apparatus which is all sufficient in determining the supply of commodities which yield their end-products of satisfaction to particular consumers or small bodies of consumers — the family, for example. But it is in the nature of things that this will not be available in regard to the extensive (and very important) groups of services which afford satisfaction to all and sundry — to use the well-known technical jargon, the case of *indiscriminate* as distinct from *discriminate* benefit : roads, bridges, lighthouses, and so on. In this sphere we are indeed confronted with the typical problem of the theory of public finance, how much to spend on services of this kind, and on whom to place the burden of the expenditure — and the market, as such, cannot provide the solution.

Confronted with this problem, certain liberal spirits, conspicuously Knut Wicksell and Erik Lindahl,[1] have suggested that it, too, can be solved on a voluntaristic basis — the basis of the famous Club State. The fundamental principle of taxation, they argue, should be proportionality to benefit received. But, of the various forms of public services provided, not all groups will conceive themselves to be equally benefited — some will want lighthouses more than others. The ultimate decision, therefore, must be a compromise, as between members of a club : one group will consent to pay its share for a service it does not greatly desire, if the other groups will consent to do likewise in respect of services from which it will benefit. Very intricate patterns of possible bargains of this sort are furnished by way of illustration.

The vision is sympathetic : at first blush the conception of the state as a club is congenial to the liberal temperament. But, alas, I fear, it is founded on illusion : its true home is not liberalism but philosophical anarchism. As Wicksell himself had to recognize, if there were no coercion behind taxation, there would be no reason why any particular

[1] See their respective papers on this subject reprinted in *Classics in the Theory of Public Finance*, edited by Musgrave and Peacock. See also the very clear statement of this point of view by Dr. Benham in his 'Notes on the Pure Theory of Public Finance', *Economica*, 1934, pp. 436-58.

individual should volunteer to pay taxes.[1]  I would not wish
to deny that, up to a point, such interpretations of the benefit
principle may point the way to the maximization of consent
and the minimization of coercion : to this extent the notion
is a useful addition to the theory of Public Finance.  But, as
I see things, to use an algebraic metaphor, there must always
be an irreducible surd of coercion in the financial arrangements of states.  Indeed, I should be inclined to argue that
it is just this element which distinguishes a state from a club,
that the one involves coercion and the other does not.  And
it is no answer to this to argue that in the end all obedience
rests on choice.  Up to a point, indeed, we may well 'consent' to be coerced when the alternative is punishment.  But
to represent this as a 'free' choice, on all fours with free
choice in exchange or production, is to obliterate the whole
distinction between freedom and coercion.  And, if this is
true, then there can be no escape from politics, even on a
benefit theory of taxation.[2]

But beyond all this, it must be recognized that any
purely voluntaristic theories of economic policy of the kinds
I have been discussing, must rest implicitly upon the assumption of a given distribution of property and income ; and
this undoubtedly involves political principles of the most
far-reaching significance.  It may, of course, be argued that
the power to influence the market to-day is the result of the
influence of the market on earlier days ; this is certainly true
and may well be thought to have important morals for
policy.  But it is not the whole truth.  For the ownership of
property and the ability to earn income are not solely the
resultants of antecedent market processes ; they are also the
resultants of the law regarding property and family obligation
and the whole system of taxation and public expenditure ;

---

[1] For an illuminating discussion of this problem, see the three articles by Paul
Samuelson, 'The Pure Theory of Public Expenditure', 'A Diagrammatic
Exposition of a Theory of Public Expenditure', and 'Aspects of Public Expenditure Theories', in the *Review of Economics and Statistics*, for November 1954,
1955, and 1958.
[2] See also the discussion of this idea in the paper on *Freedom and Order*
below.

and it would be impossible to argue that these are to be regarded as determined — or fit to be determined — by purely economic considerations. Needless to say, in any rational view of such matters, economic considerations have their place. But any suggestion that, in any realistic or normative sense, they can be said to be paramount does not seem to be tenable.

v

If these arguments are correct, it seems to follow — and here I enter the last division of these reflections — that there can be no question of a theory of economic policy which does not depend in the most intimate way upon political judgments and valuations. We must certainly hold fast to the idea of a neutral science of economics, a system of generalized description of influences and movements in the world of economic relationships. To have recognized in this connection the distinction between positive and normative judgments is one of the achievements of thought since Adam Smith and the Physiocrats; and nothing but confusion could come from any attempt to slur it over. But the idea that there can be constructed a system of prescriptions which results more or less inevitably from the results of positive analysis can involve scarcely less of a confusion: any theory of economic policy must depend partly on conventions and valuations which are imported from outside.

Moreover, as also emerges from this argument, there can be no question of circumnavigating this difficulty by the simple acceptance of some general postulate that something should be maximized — utility or the range of free choice. As we have seen, the judgment of what increases or diminishes social utility itself involves further judgments of value; and outside a framework of decisions which are essentially political, the maximization of freedom is an objective without sufficient definition. It may be very right and proper to test our conclusions by reference to ultimate postulates of this sort: I say nothing against that, although the possibility of a conflict between the claims of utility and freedom

19

suggests difficulties even here. The point is rather that, in discussions of specific problems, there is a complex of derivative precepts and assumptions which are as immediately relevant as these final overriding criteria; and that means that at almost every stage we are involved with this kind of proposition.

Let us take an actual example, the discussion of the *pros* and *cons* of the lowering of duties on agricultural imports in a régime of high protection. Now we can completely leave out of account the purely party-political aspects of this matter — whether the various effects will, or will not, benefit the party in which we happen to be interested — and I am clear that as academic economists we are usually very well advised to do so. But let us not think that, in making this renunciation, we have relieved ourselves (or somebody else) of the necessity for making any assumptions other than the desirability of an increase of social utility or the range of fulfilment of individual choice. For clearly, any change of this sort must at once affect the relative position of the domestic producers; they are worse off, the consumers are better off. How, without political criteria, are we to judge the importance of these losses against those gains?

Now your very up-to-date 'new' welfare specialist may think that he can get round this difficulty by some sort of compensation test which lets him out of direct comparisons. Put crudely, if, out of the economy to the consumers, we can compensate the producers so that they are no worse off than before, then the change is desirable: if not, not. But, even granted that this were possible — which we all know to be ten thousand miles away from practical reality — the problem of policy is not yet nearly solved. At what rate do we compensate and whom? The process of readjustment involves movement of people. Do we compensate before or after this process? If we compensate before, we run the risk of frustrating the incentive to move. If we wait till the process is over, we appear to ignore the psychological costs of movement. Furthermore, even if we postulate that the only compensation relevant to the question of the desirability of change is compensation to the absolutely non-mobile and specific productive agents or workers, we are still begging the very important question, whether, if the general rule be adopted of safeguarding the property owner or the skilled worker from all change, there is any function left for private property or private initiative. I ask such questions, not with any desire to suggest answers one way or another, but solely in order to show that answers are necessary, and that the answers which are given must, at almost every stage, involve political valuations as well as economic analysis.

I chose this particular example because, at first sight, it seems to offer an opportunity *via* the so-called compensation tests of avoiding the inter-personal comparisons which rendered politically suspect the older welfare economics : yet, as I hope to have shown, even if we approach the problem this way, we are speedily involved in further difficulties which can only be solved by appeal to assumptions which are ultimately political in nature. And, of course, if we go beyond this sort of case and consider problems of policy overtly involving considerations of distribution, problems of transfer and taxation within the community, to say nothing of the problems which arise when we condescend to the degree of reality involved by the assumption of more than one national area, the moral is even clearer. The position is quite indefensible which claims implicit prescriptive power without an extensive battery of political norms and assumptions.

But does this mean that in this field there can be no certainty, no binding body of rules on which we can hope for general agreement? Are we, as professional economists, to regard our analysis and our techniques as being as much at the disposal of ideological systems which we should regard as bad, as of those which we should regard as good? Are we in the position of the natural scientist whose discoveries may be used to destroy happiness or to increase it?

From the formal point of view I should say that our position is precisely similar — although I am fairly clear that no discoveries that we make are likely to have anything like the potential for evil as theirs. And I should certainly agree that in society, as it has developed up to date, there is in sight no very obvious resolution of ideological conflicts and consequently no very generally acceptable criteria of the political assumptions which it is necessary to make, not only in judging the results of our analysis, but even in formulating the questions to be asked. A political outlook which sets supreme value on equality will have standards of judgment radically different from one which sets supreme value on liberty. An insistence on the importance of hierarchy as such will give rise to a system of values skies apart from one which takes its rise from the maxim *la carrière ouverte aux talents*.

Nevertheless, there is perhaps a spot more hope than these propositions would seem to indicate. For, for those who are not absolutely wedded to dogma, there is probably a substantial area of valuations where adjustments can be made possible by greater understanding. If we are at all prepared to judge our standards by their consequences, then a fuller analysis may bring greater agreement. If, for instance, it can be shown that the consequences of an attempt to enforce complete equality must mean a total suspension of liberties to which most attach importance, some reformulation of the ultimate goal may seem desirable. Similarly, if it can be shown that a policy aiming only at liberty involves degrees of inequality which to many would be unacceptable, some modification of this aim may suggest itself.

Now, as I see the world of to-day, a substantial number at least of our political judgments are made in very great ignorance of consequences. Our minds are dominated by *clichés*. We judge by categories rather than by substantial implications. If, therefore, economic analysis, by pointing to the results of action rather than to action considered intrinsically, can do something to focus our valuations on real feelings and perceptions rather than on the idols of dogmatic creeds, it is perhaps possible to hope that some at least of our differences may dissolve. Clearly, this is an act of faith — and an act of faith which is not likely to have substantial realization in the near future. But it seems to me worth making. And if it proves to be justified, then we, or our successors, may perhaps claim that, although its logical priority is not in dispute, there is a real sense in which politics may be said to have been at least in part dependent upon economics.

VI

And now, finally, what of Keynes and Cournot and their respective hopes and fears as expressed in my opening quotations? I think we should agree with Keynes that, in the end, the world is governed by ideas and by little else. But I think we must note — what he actually said but what in the context is perhaps apt to escape notice — that these ideas are not only the ideas of economists but also the ideas of political philosophers, and that more often than not, as in the examples I have given earlier, it is the conjunction of the two which can be so powerful. Perhaps this is partly what Cournot had in mind when he urged that scientific arguments alone are unlikely to settle the course of events ; and, if that was so, then in that respect at least we may agree with him too.

There remains, however, still the question posed by his ultimate comparisons. Is it true, as Cournot contended, that the development of social life is like the development of language and as little affected by science as language by grammar? I doubt it. The comparison between social institutions and language is indeed a profound one and throws a flood of light upon the spontaneous elements in the evolution of both. But the comparison between grammar and science is less convincing and less borne out by experience. For while we can agree that grammar has done, and probably can do, little to promote the growth of language, must we not also contend that science — social science, the product of mind reflecting upon itself and the social universe about it — for good or for bad, can change the world, and, as our examples show, has indeed sometimes done so ?

# PART II

# 2

## FREEDOM AND ORDER [1]

### I

I should like to preface this lecture by confessing to you that I have found it very hard to prepare. As I usually find choosing a subject a matter of great difficulty and anxiety, it was with great pleasure that I accepted your invitation to lecture on a topic already predetermined, which seemed to me both interesting and important. What could be more relevant to our current problems and perplexities than the relations between freedom and order! But, as I came to reflect further, as I came to read round my subject and to collect on little slips of paper the stray thoughts that passed through my head, I began to feel that I had agreed to do something almost beyond my powers; and further attempts to organize my material have only deepened this fear. I am afraid that what I have to offer this evening must appear extraordinarily sketchy — a series of notes rather than a systematic treatment, a record of the responses of an economist to certain general problems rather than a logical build-up of social theory.

### II

Let me begin with ethical ultimates. The words 'freedom' and 'order' each appeal to our emotions. When we hear them said or when we read them, we respond favourably: we feel that they stand for something desirable. We want freedom and we want order — at least I do. Arguments on either theme can command a considerable degree of assent.

At first sight, therefore, it might appear that our central problem, the problem of the relation between freedom and

[1] A lecture delivered at the Brookings Institute in the spring of 1954.

order, was a problem of determining the proportions, so to speak, in which these two goods should be combined. Doubtless on one level that is how it looks. Much of what I shall have to say this evening will be concerned with the limitation of freedom to secure order and of order to secure freedom. There are a great many special problems that can suitably be posed in this manner.

But if, instead of describing particular tasks, we are trying to weigh final objectives, then, I think, this way of putting the problem may be very seriously misleading. For, at least as I conceive things, in the last analysis, freedom and order are not on all fours at all. They are not each ultimately desirable states to be combined in a suitable ratio in order to achieve some sort of maximum. Rather they are related to each other as end and means. I desire freedom as an end in itself. I desire order as a means to freedom.

This view is not one that is universally adopted : some of the greatest minds that have worked in this field have adopted positions that are radically opposed to it. It has been denied that freedom is good in itself. It has been claimed that certain kinds of order are intrinsically valuable. It will make my own position clearer if I set out a little the *pros* and *cons* of these opposing positions.

Take first the doctrine of freedom as an end. The stock objection to this way of looking at things is the question : *freedom for what?* Freedom, it is urged, is not something that is intrinsically good. It is a condition of action rather than a criterion thereof. A free action is good if it leads to a good end ; it is bad if it leads to a bad one.

Now it may be admitted at once that there is a point here that is well made. If describing freedom as an end in itself implied that all free acts were good regardless of their content, the position would be untenable. Clearly some free acts are good and some are bad. It is the main function of moral judgment to make just such distinctions.

But while it would be wrong and, indeed, absurd to claim that all free acts are good, I venture to suggest that it is neither wrong nor absurd to claim that, before any action can be judged to be either good or bad, it must have the quality of being free. An unfree act may lead to good results, as may a shower of rain, or it may lead to bad results, as may an earthquake. But like the rain and the earthquake, in itself it is not a suitable subject for moral judgment.

In saying this, I say nothing one way or the other on the grand question of free will or determinism. It may be that there is a sense in which ultimately nothing is free, although personally I should be a little surprised if this were so. But in the context of social ethics this is irrelevant. We may find it hard to give a definition of social freedom that is totally immune from objection. But we know in practice what it means : or at least we know the meaning of *un*freedom. We know what it means always to look over one's shoulder when one talks. We know the difference between choosing one's own way of life and living the way someone else thinks is good for us. For my purposes that is all we need to know. All that I am asserting at this stage is that only acts that are not unfree in this sense are eligible for moral classification. So that although it would be wrong to regard freedom as being in itself an ultimate good, it is an essential condition of anything that is. The creation of conditions that are free may be the creation of conditions in which good acts and bad acts are possible. But unless there is freedom, there is no possibility of good acts at all. It is in this sense that I speak of freedom as an end. It is in this sense that the prevalence of freedom is a precondition of the good society.

### III

Let me now turn to the claims of order. It is not at all impossible to understand the frame of mind in which certain patterns of social relationships seem in themselves to be good. We are moved by the spectacle of order in the universe around us. The mysterious world of aesthetic values, so elusive yet so intensely real, seems to depend ultimately upon the proper ordering of its various ingredients. It is easy to transfer such habits of evaluation to social relationships and to argue that what is good and desirable is conformity to a certain order. Plato's Republic, where the relations between the citizens are supposed to realize in themselves the idea of justice, is an example of this kind of conception. It is the recurrent ideal through history of spirits who are perplexed and shocked by the apparent disorderliness of change.[1]

We must not dismiss such views as ridiculous. It may well be that some sorts of order in adult social relationships are indeed aesthetically pleasing. But, as I see things, before they can be the subject of moral approbation — as distinct from the approbation that we give to pleasing natural objects or artefacts — they must be the result of free choice on the part of those participating. On this view there is all the difference in the world between an order that is *imposed* and an order that is *achieved*; and it is only in respect of the latter that a mature human society can be judged in terms different from the terms in which we judge the state of a herd of domestic cattle. This is not in the least to decry aesthetic values and aesthetic experiences. In the life of the individual they may well be pre-eminent — revelations of modes of being far transcending in importance the life of the common day. It is only to say that, by themselves, they are not appropriate to the evaluation of social arrangements. To value social patterns as such, whether or not they are imposed from above or freely achieved, is to commit the ethical sin against the Holy Spirit — to regard human beings as instruments and not as ends in themselves.

It is by arguments of this sort that I would seek to dispose of the purely aesthetic case for order as opposed to freedom. But, of course, even if these arguments be accepted, they do not dispose of the case that can be built up on other grounds. They do not at all dispose of what may be called the utilitarian arguments for paternalism. These seem to me to be much more formidable and to deserve somewhat fuller attention.

The case for liberty as I have presented it involves an

---

[1] See Karl Popper, *The Open Society and Its Enemies* (1950), for a masterly analysis of Plato in these terms. My discussion at this point is heavily indebted to this truly great book.

assumption that so far I have not made very explicit — the assumption, namely, that the citizens are sufficiently mature to know their own interest or to be guided towards it by reason and persuasion. Even in the most advanced society, the argument for freedom cannot sensibly be applied to the case of children or imbeciles. It would be fairly generally conceded that it does not apply in full rigour to backward adult societies. This point was well put by John Stuart Mill in his classical statement of the case for liberty, who said :

> It is, perhaps, hardly necessary to say, that this doctrine is meant to apply to human beings in the maturity of their faculties. We are not speaking of children, or of young persons below the age which the law may fix as that of manhood or of womanhood. Those who are still in a state to require being taken care of by others, must be protected against their own actions as well as against external injury. For the same reason we may leave out of consideration those backward states of society in which the race itself may be considered in its nonage. . . . Liberty, as a principle, has no application to any state of things anterior to the time when mankind have become capable of being improved by free and equal discussion. Until then, there is nothing for them but implicit obedience to an Akbar or a Charlemagne, if they are so fortunate as to find one.[1]

The argument is cogent. But it must be recognized that once it is admitted there arise very serious problems concerning where to draw the line. Who is to say at what time a child becomes capable of being guided by reason and persuasion ? When does a backward race cease to be backward ? How certain is it that all adult members of advanced communities are fully capable of reasonable action ? This last point, in particular, was seized upon by that very acute lawyer, Fitzjames Stephen, and made the basis for by far the most searching attack that has ever been made on Mill's position. He said :

> You admit that children and human beings in ' backward states of society ' may be coerced for their own good. You

[1] *On Liberty*, Blackwell reprint (1946), p. 9.

would let Charlemagne coerce the Saxons, and Akbar the Hindoos. Why then may not educated men coerce the ignorant? What is there in the character of a very commonplace ignorant peasant or petty shopkeeper in these days which makes him a less fit subject for coercion on Mr. Mill's principle than the Hindoo nobles and princes who were coerced by Akbar? [1]

I can think of various answers to this position. It could be argued, perhaps, that the degree of maturity postulated by Mill's contention is not very great; and that although beyond that point paternal control may produce immediate good, yet in the long run it inhibits further development and so prevents an even greater good. I think Mill would have argued this way, and I am sure that in many cases such a reply would be valid.

Nevertheless, if we are honest with ourselves, I do not believe that all of those who take the libertarian view would at all times wish to confine the argument for paternalism to these very narrow limits. Modern governments do many things, which, while not strictly necessary to preserve liberty, yet involve some interference with liberty, at least in the shape of additional taxation; and while we should probably condemn some, perhaps many, of these activities, it is improbable that we should condemn all of them. Think, for instance, of the use of taxpayers' money to finance some form of learning which does not pay for itself or to preserve some historical monument which, if not provided for in this way, would crumble or be disposed of for other purposes.[2] Many of the educational and cultural functions of government often involve a considerable degree of implicit paternalism; and I think we rightly regard as doctrinaire those who are quick to call them in question.

That is all very well. But if we acknowledge such exceptions, the problem presents itself with even greater insistence,

[1] Fitzjames Stephen, *Liberty, Equality and Fraternity*, Second edition (1874), p. 28 n.

[2] See the paper on 'Art and the State', below pp. 53-72, where such problems are discussed in greater detail.

where then are we to draw the line ? For although we ought not to worry too much about small infringements — *de minimis non curat lex* — yet if we have no line at all in mind, we may easily find that in admitting these small exceptions we have, so to speak, let in the whole theory of paternalism by a back door. I do not think that it is altogether an answer to say that these are problems each of which must be dealt with on its merits by good sense and long-run considerations of utility. That, in effect, was Fitzjames Stephen's answer. But without some additional safeguard, it is very easy to imagine his main argument being made the pretext for extensions of paternalism, which probably he would have been among the very first to condemn.

The right qualification, I think, is one that in fact has been provided elsewhere by Mill himself. In his *Principles of Political Economy* when discussing paternalistic intervention he lays it down that :

> . . . In these cases, the mode in which the government can most surely demonstrate the sincerity by which it intends the greatest good of its subjects is by doing the things which are made incumbent upon it by the helplessness of the public, in such a manner as shall tend not to increase and perpetuate but to correct that helplessness . . . government aid when given merely in default of private enterprise, should be so given as to be as far as possible a course of education for the people in the art of accomplishing great objects by individual energy and voluntary co-operation.[1]

That surely is the ultimate test. We can justify paternalism if it can genuinely be said to be a preparation for freedom. We can justify some limitation of present freedom if it can genuinely be shown to be in the interests of greater freedom in the future. There are obvious dangers even here : it is not difficult to think of the most disgraceful acts that it might be attempted to justify in this way. But, in principle, I think the rule is sound. At least it has the merit of involving no derogation from the ultimate case for freedom.

[1] John Stuart Mill, *Principles of Political Economy*, Ashley edition (1909), Book V, chapter xi, p. 978.

IV

Up to this point my remarks have been directed to establishing the precedence of freedom over order in the realm of ends. I have tried to exhibit freedom, if not as something necessarily always good, at least as something that is a condition of good; while I have exhibited order as instrumental. I now reach a stage where the emphasis needs to be changed, where, without regarding order as good in itself, I have to discuss it as an indispensable condition of freedom.

I take it that I do not need to spend much time in establishing the general principle that freedom in society does not mean freedom to do just anything regardless of the effect on others, but rather freedom within a code of rules designed to eliminate disharmonies. It is clear that freedom is reduced if we all consider ourselves free to behave as gangsters. Moreover, there are many forms of activity not gangster-like which if unco-ordinated or unrestrained may lead to loss of freedom. The business of living together involves an apparatus of law and order. And the provision of this apparatus and of certain other goods enjoyed in common involves contributions in cash or services in kind that are also a matter of obligation. The framing of such rules and the imposition of such levies in such a way as to create freedom rather than to destroy it, is doubtless a matter of intense difficulty; it is the grand problem of the art of liberal politics. But of their necessity in principle there is no very serious question.

There is, however, an aspect of all this, an aspect that is peculiarly germane to my general subject — which is not always sufficiently emphasized — namely, the essential core of coercion that underlies this apparatus. However much we may insist that the purpose of the state is to safeguard freedom and the good life that freedom makes possible, we deceive ourselves and run the risk of serious practical error if we do not recognize that it is *not* a purely voluntary association — that in the last analysis it involves an irreducible element of force.

It is worth while dwelling a little on this point, for it is a matter on which some economists at any rate have entertained delusions and fostered constructions that definitely conceal this somewhat unpalatable fact. There are so many social relationships that one can conceive in terms of spontaneous agreement and contract, so many complicated liens that rest entirely upon mutual benefit, that it is tempting to conceive of the state in the same way. It is admitted that we cannot think of the state as a market, giving due proportionate representation to the bids of minorities, however small and however associated. But can we not at least base our conception on the idea of a club all of whose actions are the result of mutual agreement?

Unfortunately this is not so. It is quite true, of course, that there is a sense, immortalized by Hume, in which all government can be said to rest upon consent — somebody's consent, the consent of the persons or groups of persons who have it in their power to make trouble. But it is not true, it never has been true, and it is never likely to be true that all the citizens will obey the law willingly all the time and pay their taxes as voluntary contributions. The idea of a club leaves out the essential distinction between the state and other forms of association. In the old days when migration was freer and when national exclusiveness was weaker, there was rather more plausibility for those contractual theories of government, according to which if you rejected the arrangements of one state, you transferred your allegiance to another. But they were never true for the great majority of the people; and they failed to touch the inner necessities of the situation. It is silly to say that if you hang a man or put him in prison you do it with his consent. Doubtless it should be the aim of all to see the coercive element in government reduced to a minimum, to bring it about that what is voluntarily accepted grows more and more and what is accepted only as a result of *force majeure* grows less and less. Doubtless it is supremely important to bring it about that the exercise of force is not arbitrary, that there exists a machinery for peaceful change of the government and laws (or binding conventions) limiting its scope. But we oversimplify the world and leave out an essential part of the picture if we fail to

35

recognize the irreducible element of coercion in any conceivable stable society. What is worse, we may compromise the possibilities of freedom.

We can see this very clearly if we consider the present state of international society where there is no one supreme coercive power to enforce the law among states and where in consequence there prevails not order but anarchy. It is difficult to think of anything more vividly resembling Hobbes' description of the state of nature, before law backed by force came into being. Certainly in our modern age we pass our days in 'fear and danger of violent death', and the life of man runs the gravest risk of being for this reason 'poor, nasty, brutish, and short'. Yet such is the blindness of a certain form of libertarian outlook that in just such circumstances as these, security is expected to arise from a universal perception of harmony of interests; and restrictions on sovereignty are denounced as restrictions upon liberty. Please do not misunderstand me in this connection. I have no immediate cure-all for the international chaos. I would certainly not support the creation at this stage of a world federation in which the like-minded peoples of the West were hopelessly outvoted by hundreds of millions of people who are not like-minded in this way. I do not even believe in the immediate practicability of complete federation of the Western Powers, although I myself would regard it as the most hopeful thing that could possibly happen in our time. All that I wish to do here is to illustrate the chaos of social life without a framework of law and order and the futility of arrangements that neglect the need for the essential minimum of force. We may not know how to solve our present problems. But it is at least something to recognize clearly wherein these problems consist.[1]

## V

I now approach the heart of the problem — at least as it presents itself to the economist. I have tried to demonstrate

---

[1] See the paper on 'Liberalism and the International Problem', below pp. 134-55, for extensive discussion of these matters.

the claims of freedom and the general necessity for law backed by force. I have now to ask what kind of order in the economic sphere best satisfies the criteria I have formulated.

After what I have said on the general issue, I do not think that it is necessary to spend much time on the case for freedom in individual spending. To be free within the limits of one's resources to choose between the alternatives both of present consumption and of provision for the future; I will not say that this is the whole essence of freedom, but at least it is an essential constituent. There are of course difficulties in any simple formulas in this field. There is a margin for reasonable dispute in regard to saving and accumulation. There are kinds of desirable services that for technical reasons cannot be restricted to particular consumers — the whole field of indiscriminate benefit — where we have either to go without or be content with some governmental decision involving overriding of minority preference. There are forms of private consumption that have effects on other consumers — the field of the so-called external diseconomies — where unlimited freedom may not be in the general interest. But in the main the principle is clear : the choice between existing goods and the choice what goods should be produced should be as free as possible.

Up to this point the position I have adopted might be shared by many socialists. Socialism in practice tends to the standardization of consumption and the adaptation of people to plans rather than plans to people. But there is nothing in the initial conception that implies these developments; and many convinced socialists would indignantly repudiate any such intention. The idea of freedom in the sphere of consumption is one which may be regarded as common both to liberal individualists and to liberal collectivists. It is when we come to the sphere of production that ideas are radically different.

There are two main arguments against general collectivism in the sphere of production — note, please, that I say *general* collectivism ; I have no desire to argue against all collectivist enterprise or against any conceivable collectivist experiment.

37

The first is an argument on grounds of efficiency. If the purpose of production is to serve the free choices of the citizens, then it is argued, general collectivism must fail in that by its very nature it is unable to decentralize enough adequately to fulfil this purpose. Without the degree of decentralization implied by dispersed ownership and initiative untrammelled by orders from the centre, the system must always tend either to inefficiency in meeting a free demand or to regimentation of demand in order to avoid inefficiency. This objection can be developed in different ways. It can be based, as it was based by von Mises, upon the difficulty of creating a full market system where the bids of the managers of production are limited to the requirements of a plan that is not of their making. It can be based upon the tendencies to congestion in a system that is necessarily bureaucratic. Each, I think, has a solid foundation of good sense and experience. Properly interpreted, the occasional success of collectivism in particular lines of production or in the organization of a war economy is no refutation but rather a confirmation of this view.[1]

The second argument against general collectivism is even more directly related to the central preoccupation of this lecture. It is the argument that collective ownership and control of the means of production is a danger to freedom.

It is important to realize the main burden of this argument. It is not restricted to the fact that the control by the state of the process of production is itself a limitation of the freedom of those members of society who would wish to undertake productive enterprise on their own. This is a grave limitation, and one which is probably cumulative in its evil effects; in a society in which no one can be free in this respect, it is likely that eventually no one will want to be free — which is still worse. Much graver, however, is the general limitation of freedom for all citizens except the rulers, that must necessarily arise in a society in which there is only one property owner and one employer — the state.

[1] See my *Economic Problem in Peace and War* (1947), Lecture II, *passim*.

This was well put by John Stuart Mill, who cannot conceivably be represented as being hostile to the beneficent intentions of collectivism.

If the roads, the railways, the banks, the insurance offices, the great joint stock companies, the universities, and the public charities were all of them branches of the government, if, in addition, the municipal corporations and the local boards, with all that now devolves on them became departments of the central administration; if the employees of all these different enterprises were appointed and paid by the government and look to the government for every rise in life; not all the freedom of the press and popular constitution of the legislature would make this or any other country free otherwise than in name.[1]

This point of view can be put too crudely. It is not true that every experiment in collectivism is a grave menace to liberty; it is not true that every country that has nationalized its railways lives under the shadow of totalitarian tyranny — I speak as one who is opposed to the public ownership of railways. But broadly and cumulatively Mill was surely right. The concentration of property under general collectivism must eventually be inimical to freedom. Perhaps from time to time the totalitarian night may appear to be lightened by attempts to create freedom by official orders — orders perhaps inspired by the most sincere intentions. Authors may be told not to be sycophantic, thinkers may be told to think for themselves. But you do not gather grapes of thistles; and where there is no dispersion of power, there freedom must be in perpetual danger — or else itself eventually change the system.

For both these reasons I hold that if freedom is to be preserved and progress assured, we must look outside collectivism for the answer. We must look to a system in which there is truly independent initiative and truly dispersed power. And let there be no doubt as to the reason. It is not merely that we have actual experience of something better, although I believe that in fact to be the case; it is

[1] Mill, *On Liberty*, Blackwell edition, pp. 99-100.

rather that we cannot be content without it. If we did not know a better system than general collectivism, we should have to create it. For in our generation we have seen the ghastly alternative — a mob of bemused slaves and prostitute intellectuals, mouthing the praises of the Great Dictator, an ultimate degradation of the type man.


VI

But how are we to conceive the desirable alternative, the system of diffused ownership and spontaneous enterprise? In popular discussion of these matters, it has become a habit to refer to such system as a system of *laissez-faire*, thereby, in my opinion, leading to endless confusion of thought and argument at cross purposes.

So far as its use in history is concerned, the term *laissez-faire* has a great variety of meanings. Originally, it seems to have been a protest against paternalistic regulation. It was in this form that it was used by Legendre and Gournay; and it was in this form that it became one of the slogans of the popular free-trade movements of the nineteenth century. Its development as the basis of a system was chiefly the work of the Physiocrats and certain nineteenth-century continental writers — Bastiat is perhaps the most outstanding. But it was not used in this sense by the English Classical Economists.[1] The word is only at all prominent in the work of John Stuart Mill and that in a context so hedged about by reservations that it would be quite absurd to identify his position with that of the real exponents of the let-alone philosophy. J. E. Cairnes, the last of the representatives of this tradition, in his essay on *Political Economy and Laissez-Faire* expressly repudiated the whole outlook; while Marshall, eclectic as always, but a thousand miles from the continental *laissez-faire* position, tried to give what he called 'a new emphasis to the watchword': 'Let everyone work with all his might; and most of all let the government arouse itself

[1] See my *Theory of Economic Policy in English Classical Political Economy*, especially chapters 2, 3, and 6.

to do that work which is vital and which none but government can do efficiently'.[1]  In recent years *laissez-faire* has
come to be used as a term of abuse, and totalitarian writers
have not been slow to take advantage of this to stigma-
tize any policy whatever which in any way smacks of freedom.  I await with virtual certainty the emergence of the
term *laissez-faire* collectivism to smear those socialist plans
that would at least allow some freedom in the sphere of consumption.

Thus if we take the various historical usages of the term,
we can make it mean more or less what we like ; and there
is no use in discussing it on this basis.  Indeed, there would
be much to be said for a compact, if it could be expected
that it would be honourably observed by all parties, whereby
use of the term disappeared from the vocabulary.  Still, if
we take it in the sense in which it was originally made the
basis of a general system, if, that is to say, we take it as
meaning a state of affairs in which the functions of the state
are restricted to those of a night watchman and in which the
law that is enforced consists in a very few simple prescriptions chiefly concerning property and contract, the rest being
left to spontaneous co-operation guided by the market, then
we can say that it stands for a conception differing very
greatly from the conception of a liberal order that would be
thought appropriate by those of us who follow the English
Classical tradition, suitably modified to take account of the
needs and the intellectual discoveries of this part of the
twentieth century.  It is true that both systems attach great
importance to freedom as an objective.  It is true that both
systems depend upon recognition of the possibilities of order
implicit in the institutions of property and the market.  But
their conceptions of the nature of this order and the functions
of government necessary to bring it about are so different
as to constitute two very different systems.  Let me try to
indicate what, in my judgment, are the main deficiencies of
the system, let us say, of Bastiat or Herbert Spencer, as
regards the organization of production.

[1] *Memorials of Alfred Marshall*, Ed. A. C. Pigou (1925), p. 336.

First, I would say, that a *laissez-faire* system thus conceived, enormously underestimates, if it does not entirely ignore, the whole world of desirable state action that may be described as the provision of indiscriminate benefit. It is clear that it recognized the necessity for defence and a police force, and in Bastiat there are some references to what he calls the 'common domain (Rivers, Forests, Roads)'. But when we remember that Herbert Spencer even went so far as to oppose 'State Ordered Drainage Systems',[1] it is surely clear that the scope of state action in this respect was regarded as very restricted indeed. Personally, I think that, both in regard to the advancement of knowledge and to the general appearance of things, there is still room in the twentieth century for considerable extensions of this kind of state activity. There are vast difficulties connected both with the endowment of research and with town and country planning, which in any extended treatment would require a section to themselves. But I do not think that recognition of the difficulties should preclude recognition of the strong arguments for action on quite a wide front.

Secondly, I think that this outlook almost entirely ignores the extent to which the intervention of the state is required even where the initiative in production is quite definitely in private or corporate hands. I am far from arguing that all forms of public utility regulation or franchises at present prevailing are necessary or even desirable — especially where statutory monopolies are created : current thought in this respect in my judgment is often very superficial. But it passes my comprehension to see how it could be thought that the provision of services involving long, continuous stretches of the earth's surface, excavation under public highways, regulation of the flow of large masses of water, and so on, could ever be carried to a desirable level without the special authorization and regulation by the state. Let us be quite clear about the quantitative significance of all this. If it be judged by the volume of investment it involves, I should guess that it must have absorbed at least a third of the savings

---

[1] *The Man versus the State* (1884), pp. 57-8.

of the last hundred and fifty years. Indeed, one of the most cogent arguments against general collectivism in my opinion is the argument that there is already so much that government cannot evade doing in this connection, that it is as well that it should concentrate its attention here and leave to other forms of organization, productive activities where such close association is not essential.

Thirdly, I suggest that the conceptions fostered by *laissez-faire*, both in regard to property and of contract, are far too simple — indeed, simple is not the word, *simpliste* is more appropriate. The idea that there are easily accessible clear archetypal concepts requiring a minimum of drafting ingenuity to be translated into legal instruments suitable for all times and places just does not fit the facts of life. So far as property is concerned, what are we to regard as immutable natural rights in regard, for instance, to mining rights, rivers, inventions, symphonies? The idea does not bear examination. As for contract, the belief that complete freedom should be the order of the day, including freedom to destroy freedom, is in contradiction to our fundamental principles. I am disposed to agree that a good deal that has been written about monopoly in recent literature is not only barren but also positively misleading — a good example of the danger of generalizing from rather half-baked mathematical models without referring to facts. But I still believe, as against Schumpeter and others, that there is a real monopoly problem in free societies, and that it is unwise to resign ourselves to doing nothing about it.

Finally, I think that this outlook completely side-steps all the tremendous and perplexing problems connected with the maintenance of aggregate demand. The theory of the market, as it has come down to us from Adam Smith, does indeed suggest that given reasonable stability of aggregate demand and an absence of monopolistic restriction, a system of markets and private property will turn out a flow of goods and services roughly corresponding to the demands of consumers and investors — a spontaneous order within the realm of freedom. But in itself it provides no guarantee that aggregate demand will be stable; expectations in that connection depend upon more complicated theoretical constructions. Now I am far from wishing to suggest that there can be no expectations of stability in this respect; that it is all a matter of fluke that the system is not always either at the zero of deflation or the infinity of hyper-inflation — some of us need occasionally to remind ourselves that the Great Depression was something unique in economic history. But I am quite sure that if we are in a position to expect satisfactory conditions in this respect, it must be, in part at any rate, the result of deliberate contrivance rather than predetermined harmony. There is no guarantee in the nature of things that just any spontaneous development in the sphere of money and credit will give us what we want. In fact I do not think we yet know nearly enough about these matters to be at all sure what are the best possible arrangements. But of one thing we can be fairly certain: whatever be the best institutions, whether they be one hundred per cent money, free banking on the joint stock model, or the complicated provisions of the Federal Reserve System, they are *not* the product of spontaneous initiative uninfluenced by the legal system. Where money and credit are concerned, the idea of a simple natural order is not only not plausible, it is also positively absurd.

It would be waste of time to spend further powder and shot on the conceptions of pure *laissez-faire*. Indeed, at this time of day, it would perhaps be more appropriate not so much to point out where it was wrong but rather to draw attention to the respects in which it was magnificently right — for at least its advocates were believers in freedom, at least they understood the working of the market, at least they saw through the sophistries of some paternalistic systems. But I think it is worth while to have focused thus briefly the deficiencies of their outlook if only to show by way of contrast wherein I suppose the better one to consist. I hope what I have said in this connection will at least assure you that in my conception the system of economic freedom, as Marshall called it, is not a closed system laid up in heaven, so to speak, deducible from a few simple concepts and capable of being transcribed on a couple of tablets of stone, but an evolving system, part natural growth, part artefact, continually adapting itself or being adapted to new conditions and new knowledge, whose only main general criterion is that it tends towards freedom rather than away from it.

## VII

But what about distribution? What order is implied here by the general outlook which I have tried to indicate. It is at this point that we encounter egalitarian views and are obliged to consider the claims of equality as opposed to liberty.[1]

There is clearly a certain sense in which the idea of equality is essential to the idea of a free society. The idea of equality before the law, the idea that in its dealings with the citizens, whether positive or negative, the state does not discriminate between different persons similarly situated — that is surely one of the bedrock conceptions of any society that is to be truly free. It is no accident that the more totalitarian minded of our advisers are ceaselessly attacking the principle of non-discrimination. A society in which similarly situated persons received different treatment according to their race, their colour, or their proximity to the governmental machine, would be a society in which different people had different degrees of freedom *vis-à-vis* the coercive apparatus. That would be contrary to our general principles.

But equality before the law and the administrative machine is one thing, equality in every respect relating to real income is quite another. In a society in which incentive and allocation depend on private enterprise and the market, a continuous redistribution of income and property in the interests of a pattern of equality, or something approximating to equality, is almost a contradiction in terms. Only in a

[1] On the subject matter of this section see the more extensive treatment in the paper on 'Equality as a Social Objective', pp. 73-90 below.

society in which the disposition to work could be assumed to operate entirely independently of pecuniary considerations and in which it could be assumed that the allocation problem could be solved from the centre without unfreedom and inefficiency, would it be possible to make distribution completely independent of the value of work done and to allow no inequality due to inequality of accumulation and changes in capital values. We know from Russian experience that, even under the sternest collectivism, the attempt to eliminate inequality due to inequality of pay has completely broken down. If, for reasons that I have discussed already, we decide to rely on private property as a basis of dispersed initiative and freedom, we must be prepared to tolerate the existence of some inequality arising from this source also.

This does not mean, in my judgment, the exclusion of any kind of redistribution. I do not think that the principles of a free society exclude measures for the relief of misfortune. I think the principle of compulsory contribution may be carried too far — to the sapping of independence and the undue burdening of the main body of the citizens. But, at least at this stage in the evolution of modern societies, I should regard such measures as part of the indispensable cement of social union and as conferring on most of us a positive satisfaction in the functions that are performed. Further, I do not rule out, but rather welcome, various supplements to family provisions that do something to mitigate for young people the inequality of opportunity that necessarily arises from inequality of parental position. I think that in all these matters we have something to learn from an earlier generation who regarded such measures as provisional [1] — if we may entertain the hope that eventually the great body of the citizens will enjoy the equivalent of middle-class incomes, we may surely assume that in such circumstances it would be desirable that they should assume middle-class responsibility. But that, in the present position of most Western societies, some provision of this sort is

[1] On this point, see the very powerful article, 'The Rationale of the Social Services', by Mr. Walter Hagenbruch, *Lloyds Bank Review* (July 1953).

desirable and creative of greater eventual freedom I have absolutely no doubt at all.

Finally, I wish to make it clear that I see no objection in principle to some mitigations of inequality in the interests of greater freedom. It is easy to conceive of societies in which, either as a heritage of a feudal past or the accident of the forces of the market, wealth becomes so concentrated in a few hands as to be dangerous to the political freedom of the many. I am bound to say that I think that, so far as most modern democracies go, this danger has been greatly exaggerated — the boot is rather on the other leg: the democratic levelling instinct tends to dangerous inroads on the disposition to preserve and accumulate. But where the danger exists, there the general principles of freedom would make it right to deal with it. I also think that these same principles make expedient those forms of taxation of property passing at death that tend to the diffusion of property — something very different from the effects of much inheritance taxation at present, which tends to its dissipation.

But when all these exceptions have been made, I must insist that levelling measures as such are no part of the policy of liberty. The free society is not to be built on envy; a state founded on green-eye will not stand. The position of those who say, 'let there be more equality even if it involves less wealth all round', is absolutely antithetical to the outlook which I have tried to explain in this lecture.

## VIII

One final word by way of elucidation. The picture that I have been trying to draw is essentially a picture of a society so organized that individual initiative is free without inflicting damage on others and collective action is directed to enhancing freedom rather than imposing a common pattern. Now it is fundamental to this conception that it depends upon law; that both individual and collective action should be based upon a knowledge of regulations laid down beforehand and generally applicable, rather than upon arbitrary edicts laid down to fit the circumstances of each particular case. The desirability of rules rather than authorities, to use the contrast posed so vividly by Henry Simons, is absolutely central to the main libertarian position.

Nevertheless I want to suggest that we deceive ourselves and oversimplify our position to a point at which we may expose it to ridicule, if we allow ourselves to think that all necessary rules can always be laid down in advance of the event and that nothing need be left to the discretion of legislatures and administrations. I think it is a deficiency of the libertarian case as it is often stated, that even when it explicitly repudiates the superficialities of extreme *laissez-faire*, it tends to suggest a conception of government that is too limited to the execution of known laws, to the exclusion of functions of initiative and discretion that cannot without distortion be left out of the picture. That we should have as much of legal fixity and automatic control mechanism as possible is eminently to be desired. But that we need have *nothing* but this, that all that is done by government which is not covered by this definition is either mistaken or definitely illiberal — this I suggest is not a position that will sustain serious examination.

We may note at the outset that all that sphere of governmental activity which may be described as the provision of indiscriminate benefit is *ipso facto* removed from the sphere of possible automatism. How much there should be of flood control, of smoke prevention, of the provision of civic amenities, of national parks and so on, these are problems that cannot be settled by the application of known rules; they depend essentially upon specific acts of choice. Modern legislatures and modern administrators are confronted by the urgent necessity for very many such acts.

But beyond this, and well within the sphere in which, *other things being equal*, we should hope for the predominant operation of automatic adjustment mechanisms, there are all sorts of contingencies, not in the least to be regarded as impossible, that interrupt the simplicity of the picture and call for special intervention or initiative. Take, for instance, the sphere of finance. Even if we were dealing with an absolutely closed community, it would surely be unwise, in the present state of knowledge, to assume that no situation could arise that could not be dealt with by purely automatic mechanisms; while if we are dealing with the affairs of open communities in a world of states each capable of pursuing divergent policies, I submit that it would be pure lunacy to argue that nothing could happen that could not be dealt with by pre-established stabilizers. Suppose, for instance, that some powerful state set itself, not only to absorb all the increase of gold supply but also to draw to itself by deliberate deflation all the gold already in existence. Would any responsible person be prepared to argue that the other governments should stand by with their hands crossed, confident that in the long run either the offending state would get sick of the price it had to pay, or that their own citizens would spontaneously evolve habits for dealing with a continuously shrinking volume of aggregate expenditure?

It may be said, however, that finance is in a class by itself. I admit that it offers some of the most obvious examples for the case I am trying to make. But I am afraid it does not by any means exhaust the field of possibilities. We all know that, quite apart from the provision of military forces and weapons (which perhaps can be brought under the heading of indiscriminate benefit), the fact of war, or sometimes merely near war, necessitates the application of controls cutting right across the normal reaction mechanism of private enterprise and markets. So, too, may post-war demobilization. But war and its accompaniments are not the only circumstances calling for extraordinary interventions. It is true that many of such circumstances arise because of the policies of other states — subsidy policies, state trading, and other such manœuvres; [1] to the extent that we eventually succeed in getting international affairs more subject to a commonly agreed set of rules, such contingencies would not arise. But even if we are thinking of

[1] As Adam Smith well saw. See the remarkable passage on page 41, volume ii, of Cannan's edition of the *Wealth of Nations*.

that remote abstraction — a world state or federation, it is not at all difficult to think of occasions when governmental action in supplement to or replacement of the ordinary forces of production and distribution would be called for. I will not rely on the time-honoured example of acts of God — natural disasters. To make the position clear, I am quite prepared to admit that I can easily think of inventions or even changes of taste that might produce such a situation. A discovery rendering rapidly valueless the product of populations unused to migration would fall into this category. I would say that in such circumstances it is quite possible that some intervention is desirable, if only to preserve the solidarity and coherence of the free society.

It may be argued that such an admission is dangerous, that once it is conceded that the mere fact of change may give rise to circumstances justifying the creation of controls other than the controls of the market and the legal framework, we have opened the floodgates to any sort of folly, and there is no longer any difference between our position and the position of pure interventionist opportunism. I admit the danger. But I cannot accept the implication that we should deny the facts of life and pretend that such circumstances are inconceivable. Modern liberals who appear to suggest that *everything* can be reduced to rules and automatic control mechanisms and that politics can be left to second-raters and nitwits do not make their main case more plausible. On the contrary they run the danger of bringing it into undeserved discredit.

Moreover, to admit that cases of this sort are conceivable is not to imply that they are always likely to occur ; probably most of the instances of alleged distress caused by change are best left to the existing apparatus of general relief. Nor does it imply that all kinds of measures to deal with them are equally justifiable. On the contrary, it is just at this point that the general point of view that I have been trying to develop comes into its own again as a guide to policy. That is to say, we must distinguish between interventions that destroy the need for intervention and interventions that tend to perpetuate it ; and it is only the former that are admissible. In the example that I have cited I should say that measures designed to promote mobility from the stricken area were an example of the former kind of intervention, while measures designed to suppress the invention that caused the trouble or to subsidize the price of the affected product were an example of the latter.[1]  For although with the first type of intervention, the policy adopted would tend to remove the fundamental disequilibrium, the second would tend to prolong it and even perhaps to provoke other interventions. Here as elsewhere, with all acts of government, the final test is always whether the control imposed is in the service of freedom or in the service of some other conception of society.

May I end with a quotation that will take us back to the ethical ultimates from which I started.  Most of you will remember the fine lines that Dr. Johnson inserted at the end of Oliver Goldsmith's *Traveller* :

> In every government though terrors reign,
> Though tyrant kings, or tyrant laws restrain,
> How small, of all that human hearts endure,
> That part which laws or kings can cause or cure.

I do not think that students of society in the twentieth century can go all the way with this.  We know that modern technique has made it possible for tyrant kings or tyrant gangs to create a hell permeating almost all sections of society ; and we believe we know the institutions that make such catastrophes less probable.  We hope too that our analysis indicates some forms of social order that may release forces capable of going far to diminish the worst evils of disease, ignorance, and poverty.  But if Dr. Johnson's lines serve to remind us that the goal of such efforts is chiefly negative — to reduce evil rather than create good — and

---

[1] This is a conception long contemplated in the tradition of Classical Political Economy.  See the remarkable passage from Robert Torrens' *Wages and Combination* quoted in my *Robert Torrens and the Evolution of Classical Economics*, p. 250 n.

that when everything has been done in the sphere of desirable organization :

> Still to ourselves in every place consigned,
> Our own felicity we make or find

they will still be salutary. For it is the essence of the libertarian outlook that where the true positive goods of life begin, there the economist and the political philosopher must bow and take their leave; for in that sphere they have nothing to do.

# 3

## ART AND THE STATE [1]

MY remarks in this paper will fall under three main headings.
First, I shall enquire in a general way concerning the relation between the state and contemporary art. Then I shall
discuss the special position of museums and galleries in regard
to the preservation of the art of the past. Finally, I shall
have something to say about the financial problems involved.
Throughout these divisions the discussion will be directed
specifically to the relation between the state and the visual
arts. But much of what I have to say in the first and last
sections has relevance to the relation of the state to art and
learning in general.

## II

I begin then with the general question of the relation
between art and the state. Is the encouragement of the arts
a proper function for political bodies? Is such encouragement compatible with liberal notions of the duties of the state?
When I had decided to talk about these important
questions, my first thought was to consult the sages from
whom, when young, I first learnt about the visual arts — Mr.
Clive Bell and the late Roger Fry. For, although many
things have changed since the days of their ascendancy and
some at least of their more positive pronouncements and
prohibitions seem now definitely to date, I do not think we

[1] An address delivered to the annual meeting of the Friends of the Birming-
ham Art Gallery on March 19th, 1958. It has, however, been considerably
expanded, especially in section II. Some of the illustrative figures have been
rendered obsolete by changing conditions; and, where this is so, I have
indicated the necessary corrections in footnotes and in the postscript. But I
have not altered the text in this respect, for to do that properly would be to
write another paper with a different temporal setting. As indicated in the
postscript, there has been a certain amount of improvement since 1958.

should underestimate their influence in raising general standards of taste and appreciation; although I knew neither of them in person, I shall always think of their names with gratitude and affection. I hoped, therefore, that in this connection, as in so many others, even if I did not agree with them, I should find thoughts which provoked me to further speculation.

In this, indeed, I was not disappointed. But hardly in the way I expected. Both Bell and Fry devoted explicit attention to this subject. But both reached conclusions which were quite extraordinarily negative. 'The one good thing that society can do for the artist', said Mr. Bell, 'is to leave him alone.' [1] Roger Fry went even further and argued that, under socialism, whose coming he seemed to regard as both desirable and inevitable, it would be no bad thing if all painters were amateurs.[2]

I confess that I found this attitude very surprising. I can well understand the general revulsion of high Bloomsbury from the insincerity and appalling mediocrity of the official art of the Edwardian age — up to that period an all-time low in the history of visual art in this country. I can understand, too, their very reasonable fears of the dead hand of bureaucratic organization — though recent experience seems to suggest that there may be ways of avoiding this danger. But the aggressively *laissez-faire* attitude exhibited in this connection by both these writers seems to me to pour out the baby with the bath water. For the implication that the rôle of the state in relation to art is necessarily negative seems to be untrue, both historically and in reason; and I cannot believe that, if it had been put that way, either Bell or Fry would have supported it. I just do not believe that the state has never played a positive and beneficial rôle in relation to the arts; and I see no reasonable argument to suggest that this is necessarily so, or that there are general principles implicit in the conception of a free society which would lead us to believe that it should be so.

[1] *Art*, p. 252.          [2] *Vision and Design*, pp. 36-51.

So far as history is concerned, the evidence is surely quite conclusive against any contention that the influence of states and public authorities in general has always been inimical to the arts. We know, of course, that the art of Holland in the seventeenth century and the art of France in the nineteenth were predominantly responses to demand from private patrons; and, so far as the French School is concerned, it is quite true that, for the most part, their works were spurned by the public authorities of the day. But two instances do not make an invariable rule, and the history of other periods furnishes abundant evidence of a different state of affairs. Think, for instance, of Periclean Athens or Renaissance Italy: how is it possible to imagine the public patron out of the picture in these great epochs? Admittedly, the artists of these days, as of most others, had their quarrels with the authorities who employed them. But can it seriously be maintained that Michelangelo, Raphael, and Titian, for instance, would have been better artists and would have produced more notable works of art had there been no demand for their work from the heads of states: the Popes, the Medicis, and the Venetian Senate? It is certainly possible to contend that the governments of modern times have, pretty consistently, shown a less elevated taste; and the argument is conceivable that there is something in the nature of modern democracies which inevitably precludes much hope in this connection, although I, personally, would not accept it. But what cannot be sustained is the contention that there is no form of government which can conceivably be of positive use to the arts. For that has been falsified by the facts at many times and in many places.

The argument in reason seems to me to be no less cogent.

If we begin with the essential needs of the state, it is difficult to exclude some positive influence in this respect. Public assemblies and administrative offices must be housed, schools and universities need some habitation. Is it really to be argued that all this must be catered for solely in terms of protection from the weather and the provision of proper

acoustics? Why should public buildings be the only buildings to be unadorned? Should we institute a self-denying
ordinance in this respect as a sort of penance against the
dangers of undue paternalism? As a convinced liberal — in
the philosophical, not the political, sense — I should like to
say, with all the emphasis I can command, that this is not
my conception of the appropriate conduct of a free society.
Why should it be only the unfree societies who are entitled
to make the material symbols of government agreeable?
How thankful we must be that Pericles, perhaps the greatest
of all liberals, did not conceive his functions to be thus
limited.

Considerations of this sort, I suggest, are especially
relevant to the modern situation. With the levelling of
wealth which is almost everywhere taking place, private
demand for works of art on the grand scale becomes more
and more limited. Now, quite apart from the narrowing of
scope for architectural creation which this must imply if
public works are to be of a strictly 'utilitarian' character,
are we really content that in future all painting and sculpture
should be of the dimensions appropriate to the walls and
mantelpieces of flats and suburban villas? Doubtless, if all
painters and sculptors were to be amateurs, as Fry thought
to be appropriate in such conditions, this would be a suitable
development; and if no professional talent superior to that
of most contemporary Royal Academicians were to be expected, we should not lose much by the limitation. But we
know this need not be so. Why then should we tolerate
a state of affairs in which we do not aim at the highest
excellence in the design and decoration of our public
buildings?

But, beyond this, there arises a wider question, on the
answer to which opinion is not so likely to be so united.
Beyond what is involved by the needs of the apparatus of
government, is there not a more general case for public
patronage of the arts, some general encouragement of high
excellence in culture — in the visual arts, in music, and in
the theatre?

To this question, I, personally, would answer unhesitatingly yes. And I would give this answer on the same ground as I would give support to the maintenance of sources of high excellence in learning and pure science, Archaeology, Pure Mathematics, Astronomy, for instance — subjects of no special relevance to practical affairs as such, but which impart quality and meaning to life on this planet by reason of their mere existence. And I confess that, were I not aware that there have been objectors, it would never occur to me to regard such an answer as being anything but mere good sense. When we read in Aristotle that while the state comes into being to make life possible but continues to make life good, this is just what I think he meant — or ought to have meant.

There are some, however, who regard such encouragement as a manifestation of paternalism which is foreign to the fundamental conception of a liberal state. For the state, using the money of the taxpayer, to influence in this way standards of culture and learning is for them an unwarrantable action, damaging to freedom and incompatible with the principles of true democracy. I do not know how widespread such views are to-day, but in the past they have certainly not been without some influence, and it would be wrong to believe that all who have held them have been necessarily insensitive or base.

From my standpoint, however, they rest essentially upon misconception. For the state to assume a monopoly in this respect, for it to take to itself the function of artistic dictator, would indeed be an outrage, totally incompatible with the most elementary notions of liberalism. And we can see the effects thereof, if we see the depths of banality to which the visual arts and music were reduced by the policies of Joseph Stalin. But for the state to provide encouragement and support for the arts, in a *milieu* in which there is full freedom for others to do likewise according to their fancy, so far from this being in contradiction with the principles of the free society, it is surely completely harmonious. As I see it, the situation is on all fours with the situation in broadcasting

57

and television. It was a thoroughly unhealthy state of affairs for the state, through the B.B.C., to assume an exclusive monopoly of sound broadcasting : how deeply rooted in authoritarian conception was this phase of our policy can be seen abundantly from the autobiography of its chief creator, fine public servant though he was. But for the state to be one among a number of sources of supply, its special duty to preserve and, by example, to forward the highest possible standards that seems, to me at least, to be in full accordance with the best tradition of the liberal outlook. The educational function of the state has always figured large in the philosophy of the free society — and this function is not merely a matter of teaching elementary reading, writing, and arithmetic.

As for the suggestion that patronage of this sort is an illegitimate use of the taxpayers' money, this seems to rest upon a similar misconception. Of course, if a government consistently pursues a policy in this respect which is antipathetic to the majority of the electors, then, on democratic principles, it is subject to removal and replacement by another which gives less offence : it is up to those who have positive views on such matters to seek the support of the majority by reason and persuasion. But there is nothing undemocratic in using public funds for such purposes. Only if it could be shown that there was no element of indiscriminate benefit in such forms of the educational function could such an argument begin to pass muster. But of course one of the main arguments for the educational function in general and for these forms in particular is just this, that the benefit is *not* merely discriminate, and that the positive effects of the fostering of art and learning and the preservation of culture are not restricted to those immediately prepared to pay cash but diffuse themselves to the benefit of much wider sections of the community in much the same way as the benefits of the apparatus of public hygiene or of a well-planned urban landscape. The market mechanism is a splendid thing for ministering to wants and satisfactions which can be discretely formulated. But we oversimplify and run the risk of discrediting a fundamental institution, if we claim that it can formulate demands for all the necessary ingredients of the good society. I would not say that the arts and learning can *never* flourish in a *milieu* in which they receive no support from the state. But I will say that it would be a very unusual state of affairs for this to be so: and I am inclined to argue that in most imaginable phases of the human condition, they will flourish less and bring less benefit than they are capable of bringing, unless some support of this kind is forthcoming.

### III

I now turn to the special problems of contemporary museums and galleries. So far my remarks have been addressed chiefly to the justification of support by the state for the art and general culture of the present. Now I have to concentrate chiefly on the business of those institutions whose concern is chiefly with the legacy of the art and culture of former times.

Institutions of this sort are a comparatively recent development. Needless to say, collections as such are not a purely modern phenomenon. The Royal collections on which many of the great modern galleries are founded, go back quite a long way. But the idea of the public collection, accessible to all and specifically designed to preserve the manifestations of past culture, is something which has chiefly arisen in the last two centuries; and many of the problems arising in this connection are of still more recent date.

The general rationale of such institutions ought not to be a matter of dispute. The capacity of a collection as such to yield information and enjoyment is likely to be considerably greater than that of the items of which it is composed, each considered in isolation; and the general accessibility of such collections, on a scale and in surroundings which it would pay no private enterprise to furnish, is surely something which belongs essentially to those educational functions of the state which I have discussed already. Such arguments for some collections were recognized as long ago as Jeremy Bentham who, however, while in favour of technical museums as possessing general interest and utility, was opposed to public collections of works of art and rare books on the odd ground that they were only of interest to the rich. 'The minds of the rich', he said, 'should not any more than their bodies be feasted at the expense of the poor.'[1]  But this reservation, even in Bentham's day, involved too narrow a view of the educational function; and in our own day, happily, it has ceased to have any justification, even on the plane on which it was developed.  An observer, watching the faces of the crowds which frequent our public galleries, would have difficulty in classifying the degrees of interest and enjoyment in terms of position in the income structure.

Furthermore, a provision of this sort has important functions to perform in relation to living art and culture. We live in the present but we derive from, and build upon, the heritage of the past.  It is not necessary to make the assumption of progress in the arts — an elusive, and perhaps ultimately misleading conception — to perceive that in hundreds of indirect ways the creative talent derives direction and stimulus from the matrix of tradition.  It follows, therefore, that the presence, in important centres, of collections of this kind must have a perpetually vivifying effect on contemporary creation.

It is true that this view is not always accepted.  Indeed when it was proposed to found the National Gallery, no less a voice than Constable's was raised in protest that the influence of foreign pictures would be the end of British painting; and in our own day there have been lesser artists, chiefly of Fascist inclinations, who wished to destroy the museums.  But the precepts and the practice of the best artists have usually pointed in the other direction.  The great masters of modern times, from Delacroix to Moore and Picasso, have been steeped in the great tradition; and even when they seem most unlike, their works will be found to be full of subtle reminiscences thereof.  It was Cézanne, in

[1] *Works*, Ed. Bowring, vol. ix, p. 451.

some ways the greatest revolutionary of all, who made daily expeditions to the Louvre and proclaimed as his objective to re-do Poussin after Nature. Keynes once said that he did not know which made a man more conservative, to know nothing but the present, or nothing but the past; [1] and the general verdict of history seems to suggest that this is as true of the arts as of other branches of culture. The greatest creative minds are not bound by the past, but they are aware of it and derive strength and understanding from the contact; and for the visual arts that contact is perhaps best provided by the museums. The National Gallery is not just a storehouse of dead panels and canvases: it is rather a temple of vital influences perpetually enlarging our capacities for vision and delight.

In this connection, I cannot forbear to quote the relevant extract from the speech of F. J. Robinson (later Viscount Goderich and eventually Earl of Ripon), the Chancellor of the Exchequer, at the time of the founding of that gallery; it is many years since a minister of the Crown was heard to express similar sentiments : [2]

> There remains another object to which I now wish to draw the attention of the Committee; and I think its propriety rests in some degree upon the same principle as that which I have already laid down, as applicable to Windsor Castle. In the course of the last Session, during the discussions which took place on the munificent gift of the King's Library, and on the building which was to be erected for its reception, I think a very general feeling prevailed in the House, that, under the present improving circumstances of the country, we ought not to be niggardly in matters that regarded the promotion of the arts. As a mere question of money, I do not say that objections may not be urged against any such proposition, as that which I am about to submit to the Committee. But taking a more enlarged view of the subject, looking at the intimate connexion of the arts, with all that adorns and ennobles man's nature, it appears to me to be consistent with

[1] *The End of Laissez-Faire* (1926), p. 16.
[2] But see below, p. 72, for reference to a speech by Sir Edward Boyle which may well mark the beginning of a new era.

the true dignity of a great nation, and with the liberal spirit of a free people, to give a munificent encouragement to the support and promotion of the Fine Arts. There being a fund, out of which such an object might be accomplished without any immediate pressure on the resources of the country, His Majesty's Government felt, when a short time ago an opportunity presented itself, of procuring by purchase a splendid collection of valuable pictures, that many motives of a high and liberal policy invited us to take advantage of the opportunity, for the purpose of laying the foundation of a National Gallery of works of art. Accordingly, a negotiation was opened with the representatives of the late Mr. Angerstein, which terminated in an agreement for the sale to the public of these pictures, for the sum of £57,000. I have already stated the principle on which His Majesty's Government recommended this grant; and I have not the smallest doubt, that if a National Gallery had existed in former times, the liberality of individuals would long ere this have furnished it with as fine and beautiful specimens of art, as can be found in any part of the world. Unless, indeed, I am much mistaken, there is a valuable collection at present in the possession of a high-spirited individual,[1] of acknowledged taste and judgment, which, through his liberality, would be likely to find its way to a National Gallery. Should this prove to be the case, I am sanguine in my hope, that the noble example would be followed by many similar acts of generosity and munificence: the result of which will be, the establishment of a splendid Gallery of Works of Art, worthy of the nation;—a Gallery, on the ornaments of which, every Englishman who paces it may gaze, with the proud satisfaction of reflecting, that they are not the rifled treasures of plundered palaces, or the unhallowed spoils of violated altars.

Arguments of this sort are applicable at most times and in most places. At present in this country there is, however, a further *raison d'être* for the public collection. In the past, a considerable proportion of the important artistic objects in this country have been in private hands; even to-day there remain a substantial number, as the richness of some winter

[1] Sir George Beaumont.

exhibitions at Burlington House bears evidence. But, at the present time, the burden of highly progressive taxation and the temptation of high prices in the art markets of the world are altering all that. Year by year, the great estates are being broken up by death duties; and although there is exemption in respect of works deemed to be of national importance, provided they are not sold, yet obviously, in many cases, the burden imposed elsewhere is itself an incentive to sell — there is nothing insensitive or base in disposing of, say, a valuable Rembrandt in order to preserve the home of one's fathers. If such works are bought by other domestic collectors, then, so far as the country as a whole is concerned, the situation remains unchanged, provided that there is the same degree of accessibility. But if this does not happen, then if the public galleries do not step in and buy, the works in question are exported; and since most of them are bought either by foreign galleries or with such galleries as their ultimate destination, the probability is that they are lost for ever.

Now there can be no objection in principle to the movement of works of art across frontiers. Art, thank heaven, is not specifically national; and it would ill become us in this country, who gained so much from import of this kind in earlier centuries, to argue that import by the citizens and galleries of other countries is an international outrage. I confess to a feeling of acute pain when I think of some of the migrations — the great *Feast of the Gods* by Bellini and Titian, for instance. But I do not doubt that the general culture of the West has benefited by some at least of the diffusion which has taken place.

Nevertheless, it would surely be a pity if this process were to continue indefinitely. It would be a great impoverishment of culture in this country if our remaining private stocks of great works of art were to be entirely dissipated. I cannot believe that this has been willed by the people. They may, indeed, have willed some levelling of accumulated wealth — though it is doubtful to me if they have necessarily willed it in the form in which it is taking place, *via* the estate duty, which destroys, rather than the legacy duty, which would disperse. But I doubt very much whether they have willed the transfer, to other parts, of the outstanding treasures which have been preserved in private hands. And I feel fairly confident that, if they knew that this was the by-product of the present tax system, they would be very willing indeed to take measures which, consistent with common justice to the owners, would prevent it. I should have thought that it was a matter on which all men of good-will would agree, that if, for one reason or another, it is decided to destroy or to limit any institution, then it is only sensible to provide some other means of discharging any beneficial functions which hitherto that institution has performed. Now this is exactly the position in regard to the great works of art remaining in private hands. In the past, the wealth of their owners was sufficient to keep them in the country and, in justice to the majority of owners it must be said, to make them frequently available for public inspection. But that state of affairs began to pass some time ago and is now disappearing with alarming rapidity; and if we are to retain control of this part of our artistic heritage, the state must step in and buy. Thus in a levelling age, the function of preserving this part of the national heritage, at least in so far as the greatest and most expensive masterpieces are concerned, must pass to the public museums and galleries. You may regard the change as a good thing or a bad thing, according to your ideological position. But unless you are prepared to bank on a change of tax policy sufficiently great, and sufficiently speedy, to reverse the trend, you must admit that this is the sole alternative to a further attrition of a stock of treasures which was once the envy and admiration of the world.

IV

All this is by now well known to disinterested members of the art world and some recognition thereof is beginning to make its appearance among members of the general public. What is not so generally realized, however, is the urgent

need to back this recognition with cash — with cash sufficient to cope with present prices in the international art
markets; and it is with this need and considerations relating
thereto that I wish to concern myself in this, the concluding
section, of this paper.

How best can I make vivid this problem? There are
all sorts of sensational figures. The other day, for instance,
in London, a Gauguin still-life which, before the war, might
have sold for less than five thousand pounds, changed hands
at auction for one hundred thousand. Recently in Paris a
Cézanne painting of fruit, by no means of the first order,
achieved a price of some forty thousand pounds,[1] and the
general level of impressionist works has risen in harmony. I
do not know what Colonel Maxwell's father paid for the El
Greco modello, *The Adoration of the Name of Jesus*; but I
should be surprised if it were one twentieth of the price paid
the other day to prevent its export. But these are special
instances. The best illustration I know of the general shift
in the price level of works of art is provided by contrast with
the recorded cost of all the pictures in the National Gallery
which have been bought rather than given. Up to a year
ago this was less than two million pounds. I leave it to your
imagination to conjecture what the figure would be nowa-
days if they were sold in the open market.

Why has this happened? What is it which has caused
this nearly universal rise in values? The question is worth
asking; for it is still frequently said that the present position is something exceptional — a temporary aberration of
markets which may be expected sooner or later to subside.
People have gone mad, it is said; the thing cannot last. But
although I should not be at all surprised to see considerable
changes in relative values and the price level of some artists,
or even schools, substantially less than they are now, I do
not doubt that the general rise as compared with earlier

---

[1] It should be observed that these prices relate to 1957 and before. Since
that time the tendencies diagnosed below have gathered strength and we have
seen Cézannes and Renoirs selling for over £200,000, a Rubens for £275,000
and, it is rumoured, a Van Eyck for over £500,000.

periods, is something that has come to stay and, indeed, that it is very likely to continue and even to gather strength at any rate for a period.[1]

As I see the position, there can be detected four operative influences; two very general and irreversible, two possibly of more limited duration. Let me begin with the first group which, for reasons which will soon be apparent, I will call secular causes.

First comes the diminution of supply. The stock of genuine works by dead masters is limited. As more and more of this stock passes into public possession in various countries, so the amount remaining in private hands, and so potentially marketable,[2] diminishes; and, although for a time higher prices may maintain the supply coming forward for sale, yet there is inevitably a term to it and one which approaches nearer year by year. It is, therefore, almost mathematically certain that, even if the conditions of demand were to remain unchanged, there would be a strong tendency to a rise of prices for this reason alone.

But, of course, the conditions of demand have not remained unchanged and are not likely to be so in the future. Here we come upon the second of our general causes. With the spread of education and the increase of population, interest in the arts is more widespread and intense in many parts of the world. We can see this in our own community — even if perception of the change has not yet begun to influence very much the behaviour of ministers — and in Continental Europe and the United States : the evidence in the shape of greater attendance at museums and galleries and a greater demand for the literature of the arts is there for all to see. Therefore, even if real incomes were to remain unchanged, we should expect this change of attitude

[1] What follows parallels closely a speech which I made to the annual meeting of the National Art Collections Fund in 1954.

[2] It is, of course, conceivable that examples from public collections may be sold, as happened to some of the materpieces in the Hermitage during the difficulties of the first Five Year Plan. But it is safe to say that any general movement of this sort is most improbable. Our own National Gallery is precluded by statute from any sale of this kind.

to bring about a more widespread demand for works of art of historic and aesthetic interest, both from public galleries in most parts and, where private wealth exists still on a large scale, from private purchases also. But, as we know, real income has not remained constant. In most parts of the world it has increased very considerably; and thus the initial change in relative valuations is reinforced by increased resources. In the United States, it is reinforced further by provisions in the tax law which, in contrast with the myopic logic of our own regulations, afford special exemptions to those who make cultural donations to galleries and learned institutions.

Thus, even if there were no change in the value of money, the increased demand operating on a necessarily diminishing supply would be bound to raise very considerably the height of the average price of the paintings and sculptures of dead artists.

But in fact, as we know, the value of money has not remained constant. On the contrary, in recent years it has depreciated very greatly. The purchasing power of the pound sterling, for instance, is less than a quarter of what it was in the eighties of the last century. Here, therefore, we come upon a second group of influences driving upward the levels of the art markets.

First comes the absolute change in the value of money. The influence of this is clear. Even if the particular changes in demand and supply which I have discussed already were not operative, it would seem only natural that so great a change in the level of prices in general should carry with it a commensurate change in the prices of works of art in particular. And we may assume this change to be more or less permanent. Whether or not the depreciation is eventually halted, it is improbable in the extreme that the pre-war value of money will be restored. In present political circumstances a deflation which even threatened to begin to be of that order would break any government — and, I would say, rightly so. Here then is an influence which, independently of all other factors, must tend to make prices in the art markets very much higher than in the past.

But beyond that, while there is any probability of the depreciation continuing, there is still yet another influence working in the same direction. In times of monetary instability, well-chosen works of art are a splendid hedge against inflation. For, like jewels and certain kinds of real property, they tend to keep their value without much trouble of management and their prices are not subject to the same political risks as the prices of ordinary shares. Hence, at such times, there arises a speculative demand from those who foresee further decline in the value of money which reinforces the museum and private demand which I have discussed already.

Clearly this would cease, if inflation were to cease and if investors were convinced that it would not begin again — although speculation in anticipation of the increasing disparity between supply and demand would continue. And to the extent to which it ceased, there might be some reaction in art prices. But, if I were a dealer in these markets, I should not set much store by this, partly because I am very sceptical indeed of the will of modern governments to take the necessary measures to prevent inflation and to maintain them after the moment of crisis has passed, partly because I believe that the operation of the permanently acting or secular causes would be strong enough very soon to offset any little setback of this sort. I hope therefore that I have proved that what with one set of influences and another, there is no likelihood whatever of a substantial lowering of levels already achieved. Any hope of a return to a 'saner' pre-war normal is founded on a failure to understand what is happening in the world.

But if this be true, it follows that if the museums and galleries are to perform their proper functions they need adequate funds. But these, unfortunately, they do not have. It is no exaggeration to describe their present position in this respect as pitiful and a disgrace to civilized standards. The National Gallery purchase grant is £12,500, a sum which, at present prices, with luck would enable the acquisition of one good example of the major impressionist masters —

to name a school in which the collection is conspicuously lacking — every five years or so.[1] It is true that it is possible to make application for supplementary grants and that, in recent years since the publication of the Waverley Report, such grants have occasionally been forthcoming. But the success of such applications must always be a somewhat chancy business, depending to some extent at least on the political mood of the moment; and the meagre dimensions of the recurrent provision must make any systematic purchase policy quite out of the question. If it is realized that this provision is only £2500 more than it was in the early eighties when its purchasing power in terms of cost-of-living commodities was perhaps four times as great as it is to-day, and its purchasing power in terms of old masters very much more than that, it will be seen how little public policy has kept pace with changing conditions of the market; still less with the desire of the general public for improved provision in this respect.

Why is this? I observe in some quarters a disposition to put the blame on officials. But this is completely misplaced. Those of us who have to deal with the relevant departments, know that the officials concerned are at least as sensitive and cultivated as their critics and very often considerably more so. But no responsible official is going to commit his minister to policies he has not approved of; and, the more he privately sympathizes with the arts, the more scrupulous he is likely to be in refraining from letting his personal predilections influence his discharge of his official duties.

In other quarters the blame is said to be with the House of Commons. It is argued that ministers will not do more because the House of Commons will not let them. In the distant past, I suspect that there may have been something in this diagnosis: when the Vendramin Titian was bought for the nation, just before the First World War, there seem to have been some protests against this use of public money. But there has been nothing of that for many years; and,

---

[1] It should be noted that this estimate related to 1958 prices, since then the sum in question would have become very much more inadequate.

when the government has made grants for extraordinary purchases, so far as I am aware, it has received nothing but approbation. I cannot believe that it is the House of Commons which is an ultimate obstacle to change.[1]

Nor can I believe that there is any substantial opposition among the general public. Of course, the philistines will always be with us; only a year or two ago a prominent industrialist who, so far as I know, has never given a penny to the arts, protested at the grant made to assist the purchase of the El Greco. But I think there is plenty of evidence to show that in general the public is ahead of its masters in this respect and would greet quite massive increases in the gallery grants, not merely passively, but with positive approbation.[2]

No. According both to the theory of the constitution and the facts of the contemporary position, the responsibility for the present disgraceful state of affairs rests fairly and squarely with ministers. *Noblesse oblige*: it is the duty of their exalted position to give a lead in matters of this sort; and there is every reason to believe, that if once they could screw themselves up to making what ought to be, for them privately, a pleasurable recommendation, then so far from making themselves unpopular, they would win almost universal applause.

But, it may be asked, are they justified in doing so at this stage in the economic history of the country? Is it not a fact that the inflation from which we have been suffering for the last eighteen years has as its fundamental cause an excess of expenditure in relation to the value of the national product at constant prices? Does not the recommendation of more money for the museums and galleries and more money for culture and learning in general run exactly counter to the policies of prudence in this respect?

[1] This represents a change of view from my address to the N.A.C.F. when I was disposed to put more blame on the average M.P. By the time this address was delivered I had come to believe that ministers with courage have little to fear in this respect; and subsequent history has confirmed this view.

[2] As indeed happened, when the grants were increased the year after this address was delivered. *See* the postscript below.

The question is pertinent; and, as an economist, obviously, I must face it. But I have no doubt whatever of the answer. It is quite true, in my judgment, that we have been spending too much in the aggregate. The excess can, perhaps, be exaggerated, but there can be no doubt of its existence. To prevent the inflation, therefore, it is desirable that we should spend less, not perhaps absolutely, but certainly in relation to the increase of the product. And this may well be held to imply greater prudence in public finance generally.

But it does not, in my judgment, imply that we should spend less on culture and learning, in relation to which, on any comparative standard, our spending is so much in arrears. *The necessity to curb spending in general does not in the least imply a necessity to apply the curb equally in all directions.* In private finance, if a man has been overspending on orgies, so that his total expenditure has to be reduced, that does not mean that he should not increase his expenditure on his eyes and his teeth, if his spending on these in the past has been deficient; it only means that there have to be further balancing cuts elsewhere.

And that, as I conceive it, is typical of our present position as a nation. If we wish to avoid further decline in the value of our money we have certainly to moderate the growth of aggregate spending. But it would be folly indeed if this necessity were to lead to further stinting of those sectors where in the past and up to date our expenditure has been so inadequate. Our position in this respect is a serious distortion of values. We have starved expenditure on the arts generally while we have allowed it to run to disproportionate lengths elsewhere. This surely shows itself without any room for doubt if we look at the figures: we pay up to three hundred million pounds in subsidies to various branches of agriculture, to say nothing of other subventions to high-cost enterprise at home and dubious connections abroad. Can it seriously be argued that, if such subsidies were to be halved, we could not spare a million or two from the savings for the galleries and the arts generally?

And that, as I see things, is the order of magnitude of the problem. To put the national galleries and museums in a position in which they can make appropriate additions to their collections, to remove the shadow of bankruptcy from the national opera and ballet and to provide a proper foundation, both for the activities of the Arts Council and of the British Academy, in present conditions, would certainly not involve at the outside more than an additional two million pounds to the total of public expenditure. It is difficult to believe that within a total expenditure of some five thousand millions, there are not economies available which would permit such an expansion without further increase of inflationary pressure.

## POSTSCRIPT

In view of what is said above about the attitude of ministers, it is only right to add that on January 22nd, 1959, Sir Edward Boyle, the Financial Secretary of the Treasury, speaking for the then Chancellor of the Exchequer, Mr. D. Heathcoat Amory (now Lord Amory), announced an increase in the National Gallery grant from £12,500 to £100,000, together with smaller increases to the Tate Gallery and other institutions; and that since that time the National Gallery grant has been raised to £125,000 and special grants have been made in respect of purchases of works by Uccello, Rembrandt, Gainsborough, Renoir, Goya, and others.

Such increases, although to some extent defeated by the continued rise in the art markets and still quite insufficient to afford scope for adequate filling of gaps in the collections, are of such a nature as to lead to the hope that those who rule over us are at last beginning to slough off the mentality of the earlier years of this century and reconstruct their scale of priorities on lines more in harmony with the standing of a nation which, for all its misfortunes, is still one of the leading repositories of the culture of the West.

# 4

# EQUALITY AS A SOCIAL OBJECTIVE [1]

## I

BEFORE offering my contribution I should like to congratulate the Group upon its choice of subject for this series of discussions. Equality is a catchword of the day; the levelling spirit is a characteristic of the age. Other ideas which were part of the great leftward drive have been realized or have lost their attractive power. The gilt is off the nationalization gingerbread. But not so with the idea of equality. Although, as I shall try to show, in some respects we have gone as far in that direction as a great many members of the left would, in their heads, judge to be desirable, that idea still retains its ascendancy over their hearts. Socialism is about equality, we are told by Professor Lewis. Mr. Kaldor's extraordinarily interesting book, *An Expenditure Tax*, is, to some extent at least, inspired by the same impulse. Equality as an objective still holds the field as one of the main issues of our time. Indeed, in some circles it is the basis for a sort of snobism; if you do not subscribe to the levelling slogans, you are in some sense morally inferior.

Now, if we are to discuss this issue in a realistic spirit, it is necessary to make distinctions. Equality as an objective may mean quite a number of different things; and unless these are clearly separated much confusion and argument at cross purposes is possible. It is very easy to generate an enormous head of emotional steam in favour of one kind of equality by arguments which are only relevant to another. For instance, it is not at all difficult to find people who speak

[1] This is the substance of an address to the Bow Group which, during the winter 1956–57, held a series of discussions on Equality. A somewhat shorter version appeared in *Crossbow*, vol. 1, no. 1. Autumn 1957.

as if the arguments against meting out different sentences to different people according to their race or the colour of their hair or skins furnished conclusive grounds for preventing one man from earning more than another. If you hold that it is unjust to prevent women entering learned professions on the same terms as men, you are expected, by that token, to believe also that it is unjust that different persons should own different amounts of property.

As I see things, we need therefore, from the outset, to distinguish between three very broad conceptions: equality before the law, equality of opportunity, and equality of income and wealth. In what I have to say here I shall be concentrating mainly on the last of these and its appropriate sub-divisions. But first I should like to say a word or two about each in regard to its status in the general debate.

## II

To begin, then, with equality before the law. I take it that, before a group such as this, there is no need to argue at length its general desirability. It would be going too far to say that, since the defeat of the Nazis, it is nowhere a controversial issue; for there are still substantial areas where gross inequality in this respect not only still exists, but is also the subject of passionate intellectual — or would-be intellectual — apologia. I am sure that Dr. Verwoerd does not believe in this kind of equality. And even in the detailed working out of our own administrative arrangements, it is not difficult to think of cases where different people similarly situated have been the subject of different treatment — the whole sordid history of the anomalies of rent restriction, to the removal of which this group has made such a notable contribution, is full of examples of this kind. But I think it would be legitimate to say that, in this country at least, among men of good will, the general principle is not likely to be called in question.

Nevertheless, it is perhaps just as well to state explicitly the grounds of this belief; for it is extraordinary how much muddled thinking surrounds it. Therefore, let it be said, as distinctly as possible, that it does *not* depend in any way upon the assumption of any kind of biological equality. Neither plants nor animals reveal equality within species; and it would be very extraordinary if the race of humans were to be an exception to this rule. And in fact common experience tells us that it is not so. We may well ascribe many differences between adults to nurture rather than nature; and, as I shall argue shortly, we may resolve to do all that can reasonably be done to eliminate the causes of such inequalities. But I fancy that we deceive ourselves if we believe that these account for all, or even the greater part, of the actual differences we see. As every teacher knows, not all the education in the world, from the cradle onwards, will make firsts or even upper seconds of all his pupils : it is utterly amazing to me how it could even be thought other-wise.[1] If the entitlement to equal treatment before the law depended upon potential intellectual equality to the best, or even the average, of the human race, how many very deserving people would be left out!

No. The case for this kind of equality is, *not* that all apparent differences are artificial, but rather that the exis-tence of law is a fundamental condition of a free, as distinct from an arbitrary, society, and that physical and intellectual differences are no justification for unequal treatment in this particular connection. The difference between Einstein and the hall porter affords no ground for treating them differently in regard either to punishment for crime or enforcement of contractual obligations. When Paul III, after hearing report of one of Cellini's more atrocious misdeeds, is said to have said : 'Learn that men, such as Benvenuto, unique in their profession, are not subject to the laws',[2] he was enun-ciating a principle which is the exact contrary of the basis of

---

[1] Yet both Adam Smith and J. S. Mill did think so. Adam Smith thought that at birth there was little difference between porters and philosophers (*Wealth of Nations*, Cannan's edition, vol. i, p. 17). J. S. Mill thought that his own intellectual quality was entirely due to the education he had received from his father. *Autobiography*, World's Classics edition, p. 26.

[2] *Memoirs*, Benvenuto Cellini, Everyman edition, p. 113.

a liberal society. How are we to tell which men are, and which are not, to be treated as 'not subject to the laws'; and who is to bear such momentous responsibility?


### III

When we come to our next general conception, equality of opportunity, the position is not so simple.

I think that most of us would be prepared to agree that, in itself, equality of opportunity is a very desirable objective. We should certainly think that it was most undesirable for a young person to be denied access to particular employments by some statutory or caste limitation; for that would offend against the fundamental requirement of equality before the law. And I imagine that most of us would agree that it is an unfortunate thing if, by reason of family circumstance, one who is otherwise well equipped, is denied a chance to make good in competition with his fellows. We regard such a state of affairs as ethically undesirable; moreover, we regard it as economically inefficient, in that it does not make the best use of scarce talent. Most of us are prepared to see quite extensive action by the state — more extensive indeed than takes place at present — to supplement family resources and family stimulus and create the conditions for *la carrière ouverte aux talents*. Those of us who spend our lives as teachers know well that this is one of our primary functions.

But while we regard it as desirable in itself and as a thoroughly worth-while objective of policy, I am confident that a good many of us, at least, are not prepared to make it a *sole* objective. We want to see greater equality of opportunity. But we are not prepared to sacrifice everything else in the world to secure a complete realization of this ideal.

It is worth while spelling this out a little; for I think it points to a very important distinction of attitudes. It is plain, is it not, that even if there were no differences in pecuniary advantage between the position of the children of different families, there would still prevail marked differences as regards advantages of atmosphere and enlightenment. The children of happy and sensible parents will usually have a better chance than the children of unhappy and stupid parents. Yet how many of us would be willing to destroy the institution of the family to rectify this inequality? Plato was: as you know, he was prepared to take infants from their parents at birth in order to eliminate any danger of unequal treatment. But the majority of even dyed-in-the-wool collectivists have hesitated to follow him thus far. They have normally been content to assume that, in this respect, they could both have their cake and eat it.

The abolition of the family is an extreme case; and it would be a waste of time to pursue it further. But similar conflicts of objectives may arise in connections which have much more practical significance. Thus, even if there is what most of us would regard as adequate supplementation of family resources, there can be no doubt that it remains an advantage to have parents who are well off rather than parents who are not so well off. Now to a convinced collectivist this is yet another reason for a general approach to equalization of property and wealth. But those who, for other reasons, do not believe such equalization to be desirable, will not necessarily be moved for *this* reason to go further in this direction. They will say: we believe in such an approach to equality of opportunity as may be secured by reasonable supplements to family income; but we are not prepared to paralyse the whole apparatus of incentive and accumulation to eliminate such inequalities as remain when this has been done.

It is clear, therefore, that while there may be general agreement on the desirability of the end in itself, there is still considerable room for disagreement on the lengths to which we are disposed to go to achieve it in competition with other desirable ends.

### IV

When we come to our third basic conception, equality of income and wealth, matters are on a still different footing. Here it is not, as in the case we have just discussed, a matter of probable agreement on a general objective, but disagreement on the lengths to which you should go to achieve it; it is a matter, rather, of an objective whose intrinsic desirability may well be called in question by people who are quite as intelligent and sensitive as those who support it. You may not regard equality, either of income or of wealth or of both, as having in itself any strong claim on your sense of political obligation or expediency.

It will be well to split this matter up into appropriate sub-divisions in order to examine it in proper detail.

(a) Let us begin with equality of income; and to eliminate all extraneous considerations, let us concentrate on income from work. 'Unearned' income, or income from property, can more conveniently be dealt with when we are considering equality of wealth.

I wonder how many people at the present day do in fact regard strict equality of income from work as an objective which we should wish to realize, even if it were practicable. It is true that, in the past, quite a substantial number have adopted this attitude. When I was young and the hopes based upon the Communist revolution in Russia were at their height, I am sure that many would have formulated their ideal thus; and Bernard Shaw (who, incidentally, spent his last years refusing to increase his dependants' wages to keep pace with the cost of living because he thought he himself was being taxed out of existence) argued strongly that way. But much has happened since then; and I suspect that the number of supporters of exact equality — whatever that may mean — has somewhat diminished.

Speaking for myself, I must confess that I do not find it acceptable, either from the point of view of expediency or from the point of view of ultimate ethics.

From the point of view of expediency it is surely clear that a system which guaranteed the same reward to the industrious and to the idle, to the clever and to the stupid, would be a system which would be very much less productive than, in our present state of comparative poverty, any sensible person would regard as satisfactory. I am not in the least arguing that the pecuniary incentive is the only incentive; I am not denying that scientists and social reformers and others whose product is of great importance do much without much regard to financial reward. But I am arguing that the great majority of jobs have not such intrinsic interest and that you cannot assume that the workaday business of the world will get done very well without some connection, direct or indirect, between effort and reward. I think that the experience of the Russian experiment shows that this is at least as true of collectivist societies as it is of societies based on private property and the market.

But further, from the point of view of ultimate ethics, I do not find the objective at all compelling. I really cannot see anything particularly ethically attractive in a total divorce between earnings and the pecuniary value of contribution to the social product; and I find something positively incompatible between the objective of equal opportunity, which I support, and the objective of equal reward, which I reject. Equal opportunity to win *equal* prizes — has that really a very strong appeal to the candid intellect or the fastidious social conscience?

(b) Let us turn then from earnings to wealth and the income which may accrue from the possession thereof. What of the egalitarian ideal here?

Now nothing can be more certain than that, if any private accumulation out of earnings be permitted, there will emerge some inequality of possessions; and further that, if investment of such accumulation takes place, there will arise some inequality of income therefrom. This would obviously happen even if all private property reverted to the state at death. Different people have different *dispositions* to save. If there is inequality of earning, different people will have different *ability* to save; and once saving has taken place, different forms of property will undergo different vicissitudes of valuation. If there is transmission of property at death, then there will be further possibilities of inequality: different people will enter into different inheritances. But the main point should be clear: once private property is allowed at all, some degree of inequality is more or less inevitable. Equality all round all the time would be the most unlikely fluke. If, therefore, you believe in private property on any substantial scale, if you think, as I do, that it safeguards liberty and decentralized initiative, you are *ipso facto* committed to a social objective which involves some negation of the objective of equality.

It is considerations of this sort which so frequently have led thoroughgoing egalitarians to advocate the complete or the virtual abolition of private property. Whether or not total collectivism would secure a better organization of production, at least, they argue, it would prevent the existence of inequality of private wealth. Let justice be done even if the heavens fall. If, however, you believe that collectivism of this sort will not be very efficient, still more if you believe that such a concentration of power in the hands of the rulers of monolithic states means the elimination of political liberty and the probable disappearance of spontaneity and truth — a fear which has much empirical verification — you may easily think the remedy to be much worse than the disease, and revise your views regarding economic equality as an objective.

All this, however, relates to logical extremes. In fact at the present day it is doubtful whether the majority of the left would be willing to shape their ideals so severely. They may continue to get a considerable release of the soul from the reiteration of the traditional slogans. But if they are challenged as I have challenged them now, of course they will strongly reproach you for assuming that they ever meant anything so crude. They are prepared to admit the necessity of some connection between earnings and output. They will admit the necessity, even under collectivist institutions, for some degree of private saving. Even in Russia some degree of transmission of property at death is permitted.

So that in the end the problem of practical politics, at any rate in the contemporary situation, is not a matter of total equality or not, but rather how much equality to aim at, or how much inequality to permit, in regard to particular kinds of income or wealth. This is perhaps a less exciting question. But, as we shall see, it affords ample scope for discussion and disagreement.

V

Before examining particular cases, let us pause a little to clear our minds about the general aspects of the more limited objective now in view. Given that complete equality of income and wealth is — to use Bentham's phrase — chimerical and undesirable, to what extent do we support the *reduction* of inequality as a general objective?

This is not a question to which cut and dried answers are possible in the sense in which we could give cut and dried answers to our earlier questions. This is because, while equality in this sense is a conception of a unique relationship, there are almost an infinite variety of possible patterns of inequality — and the probability is that you will regard some as tolerable and others as not.

Nevertheless, I think it is not impossible to reach certain general positions, testing our reactions as we go by reference to contemporary reality.

In the first place, I would say that, in an economy such as ours, most of us would approve of measures designed to relieve extreme poverty and distress. We approve too, for reasons I have already discussed, of extensive measures designed to increase equality of opportunity by supplementation of family income for purposes of education and health. All such measures have a tendency to greater equality of income per head; and although this is not necessarily their *raison d'être*, we certainly do not disapprove of them for this reason. Needless to say, levelling-*up* measures of this sort present great problems in detail about which men of good-will may easily differ. But the desirability of the general tendency is not seriously questioned.

It is far otherwise when we come to measures which have the specific intention of reducing inequality by levelling *down*. On this matter, I think, there is considerable clarification to be achieved by some brief meditation on the general idea of progressiveness in taxation.

As I see it, this idea can be recommended on either one of two grounds — as a means of sharing a common burden or as a means of reducing inequality. These grounds are quite distinct and the difference between them involves a whole world of difference as regards political attitudes.

Thus the idea of progression as a means of burden-sharing seems to me quite acceptable to a non-collectivist attitude. Given the usefulness of the public expenditure to be financed, I see no objection in principle to sharing the burden in this way. Even the firmest supporters of the proportional principle — J. S. Mill, for example — are usually prepared to concede an exemption limit — and of course proportionality above such a limit arithmetically involves general progression. Progression of this kind and for this purpose seems to me good ethics and common sense ; and to support it for this reason does not in the least rule out discussion of what degree of progressiveness is expedient in the light of considerations of incentive.

In contrast to this, progression specifically designed to reduce inequality seems to rest upon a much more dubious footing.

I do not think we should say that in principle this is *always* unacceptable. It is not impossible to think of patterns of inequality so gross that some reduction by way of taxation is politically desirable. But in general I confess that the idea does not have for me any strong ethical compulsion — rather the contrary. The levelling-down impulse seems to me to be often associated with a state of mind which I find ethically unpleasing. The citizen, still more the politician, who is always thinking of relativities is not a particularly edifying spectacle. What is there specially admirable, I ask, about taking away proportionately more of a man's earnings just because the work he does happens to be more highly paid ? Is there not something slightly incongruous about society offering, through the market, one rate of pay, and then, through the tax machine, reducing it, not just incidentally in the course of financing necessary services, but deliberately and of set purpose because the rate is thought to be too high ?

This is not to say in the least that I attach ultimate importance to the values of the market. I do not think, for instance, that a member of the academic profession is ethically or socially inferior because his salary ceiling is usually under, say, £3000 a year, while film stars and boxers can sometimes make thirty or forty times that amount. But I do not think he should resent their being able to do so. And my impression is that there is not all that resentment among the wage-earning part of the electorate. It is the finical intellectuals, often themselves living comfortably on inherited investment income, who are continually looking around for something to worry about.

Beyond that, since I am revealing to you a somewhat unregenerate frame of mind, I might as well confess that I take no pleasure in the more general effects of the degree of progression now prevailing. Some, whom I respect, may enjoy the idea of the tremendous reduction which has taken place in the numbers of higher incomes. But if I think of it in terms of concrete results, the appearance of the consumption pattern, the colour of town and country, the narrowing of the scope for variety and experiment, I do not share this feeling. I do not suggest for a moment that the finer values of civilization depend only on the expenditure of the higher income groups : that would be not only an oversimplification but even a positive misrepresentation. But a good deal still does so depend ; and I view with some apprehension the continuance of a state of affairs where the sources of private patronage for the more unusual and unpopular forms of art and learning have reached so low an ebb as they have to-day. At present levels of productivity at least, there is a certain drabness implicit in the operation of the levelling process.

VI

Let us now address ourselves to specific tendencies and problems. So far as income is concerned — there will be more to say of wealth hereafter — I am fairly clear that not much more levelling is politically practicable in this country. Surtax rates in the upper reaches are almost at the limit of levelling vindictiveness — you cannot take much more than nineteen shillings in the pound. And below these levels, in a society increasingly dependent on managers and technicians, the position is already politically awkward. Indeed, if you look at comparative graphs of direct tax rates in this and other Western countries, it is clear that we have gone farther down the egalitarian road than any other important country — and I, for one, should be inclined to predict some eventual reaction. It is difficult to believe that differential incentives can be maintained so much less than elsewhere under capitalism — to say nothing of Soviet Russia.[1]

The main proposals for further change which come from the egalitarian camp relate to expense allowances and to capital gains.

So far as expense allowances are concerned, my attitude is one of some reserve. I do not doubt that there are abuses — although the extent and area can be considerably exaggerated — and in principle this cannot be approved: it offends against one of the good canons of equality — equality before the law. But it is surely very obvious that, in part at any rate, the root cause of the abuses is to be found in the penal tax-rates. The majority of men are not angels; if they feel they are unjustly dealt with, they will lose their scruples against acting unjustly. This certainly is true of wage earners. I see no reason to be surprised that it applies also to business executives.

The position as regards capital gains is more difficult. I do not see any justification for denying that, in principle, the immunity of capital gains under our tax law is something of an anomaly. Nor, in the light of American practice, is it reasonable to argue that taxation of capital gains is incompatible with the efficient working of an individualist society. But I should be sorry to see the anomaly removed while our

---

[1] I have left this passage as it was written in 1956. Since then the prediction has begun to be justified.

general rates of direct taxation remain so high. The prospect of capital gains is one of the incentives which are still an effective spur to enterprise. And while it is difficult to over-state the administrative nuisance which would be involved in bringing capital gains into our tax system, it is very easy to exaggerate the yield. Extensive capital gains of the kind we have seen in recent years are essentially a by-product of inflation. Get rid of inflation, administer the system with equity, and I suspect it might well be thought that financially it was not worth the candle.

In brief, while I am sure there will continue to be a good deal of sound and fury on the income front, I do not think that we are likely to go much further in the way of general levelling. But, of course, from my point of view, that is not enough. From my point of view some *de*levelling is desirable. The present degree of progression is too great. Present incentives are not sufficient to secure a desirable rate of increase of productivity.[1] Talent tends to migrate. It is obvious that we are not going to return to the easy conditions of earlier periods. But some reversal of present trends seems to be called for.

## VII

When we turn from the field of annual income to that of ownership or wealth, we are confronted with a very different situation. We have seen already that the non-collectivist is unwilling to abolish private property, either in the interests of greater equality of opportunity or in the interests of pre-venting inequality at all. But it is not true that he is unwilling to do anything at all to affect the pattern of distri-bution. The fact that human beings die and that the trans-mission of their property at death necessarily involves very complicated legal arrangements, offers an opportunity for

---

[1] The disincentive effects of high marginal rates are sometimes called in question. But this does not seem to me to make sense. If we could not argue that it made no difference if the marginal rate were 20s. in the pound, so that there was *no* reward for additional risk and effort, why should we speak as if the position is so radically changed when the residue from a pound's worth of earnings is 6d. or 1s. ?

producing modifications of ownership which need not blunt unduly either the incentive to work or to save, but which, by a gentle and continuous process, may produce a desirable redistribution. The great social philosophers of the nineteenth century, who worked out the *rationale* of a free enterprise system based on private property and the market, themselves conceived this possibility and laid some emphasis upon it. A tax upon inheritance, graduated according to the size of the legacy, would involve a strong incentive to the diffusion of property; the more a testator divided his estate, the less total tax it would have to bear.

Such an arrangement seems to me to have much to recommend it. Far from destroying the institution of property, it tends to sustain it by causing property to be more widely diffused. And by causing it to be more widely diffused, it tends also to increase equality of opportunity without imposing limitations on the area of ownership or disincentives to work and save. It is surely a plan which is in full harmony with the spirit of a property-owning democracy.

But it is not a plan which is at present being carried out. Death duties at the present time are based, not on the size of the legacy received, but rather on the size of the total estate of the testator; and at present rates of taxation, while they certainly have the effects of destroying large accumulations, they have no effect whatever in promoting their diffusion, save in so far as they stimulate gifts *inter vivos*. The main effect of estate duty on the present scale is to transfer property to the state, which treats it as current revenue — which is the reverse of what a non-collectivist would wish. It is difficult to exaggerate the cumulative influence of this continuous attrition. It is the great revolution of our time — a revolution under anaesthesia.

I confess that I have never been able to understand why Ministers who are not Socialists have never done anything to alter this system. It certainly cannot be said that the alternative plan is administratively impossible, since for years, in a small way, it was part of the system. Admittedly

86

it is somewhat more difficult to administer. But, given the minimum *desideratum* of practicability, the criterion of policy is not administrative ease; rather it is conformity to the wishes of Ministers and the broad objectives of social policy. Nor should there be any fear based upon considerations of general financial stability. At present rates, the estate duty must be paid overwhelmingly out of capital; any fall of tax receipts which was due to assessment on the new basis, would mean chiefly a release of savings for other purposes. There can, therefore, be no reason, save an utter indifference to the long-run effects of day-to-day policy, which has prevented non-Socialist Governments from making the change.

VIII

In conclusion, may I say one more word about tendencies and the climate of opinion. Much of my analysis this evening has been negative and critical. Does this mean that, whenever I hear a man praising the objective of equality in general terms, I am automatically out of sympathy?

Not at all. Equality before the law is one of the most precious elements in the Western tradition. It was achieved by our forefathers only after long and bitter struggles; and the practice of the totalitarian states of our own age shows that we can by no means afford to take it for granted. Equality of opportunity is a fine objective — spacious, generous, life-creating. The fact that we are not prepared to jettison everything else to get it, does not mean that we do not value it, or that we are not prepared to strive most earnestly to achieve it in a less destructive way.

For the rest, in the sphere of income and wealth, we may oppose, as I most certainly oppose, the prevalent tendency to level down just for the sake of levelling. But if we are to be fair, we must recognize that it does not all spring from envy and resentment, powerful and widespread as these motives may be. A sensitive man will regret the false values which are often associated with inequality. A man of liberal spirit will find his greatest fulfilment in the society of his

G

equals — or his betters. That men should treat him as a superior is something that he will not want — rather the contrary; and he will instinctively dislike anything which tends to artificial hierarchy.

All of this, I think, should command our sympathy and understanding. The difference between those of us who reject the collectivist solution and those who support it *for these reasons*, is not that we do not share their distaste for the false values, but rather that we think they are better eliminated another way. In our conception, the things which men of good-will on both sides deplore are better dealt with by attacks on particular abuses and by remedies for particular deficiencies, than by general solutions which, however laudable the intentions behind them, would have the effect of clamping society into a strait-jacket in which just those virtues which we most seek to foster would have the least chance of survival.


# A NOTE ON THE TAXATION
# OF MARRIAGE

I am tempted to add to the general reflections on taxation included in the above paper a few paragraphs on the tax on marriage involved in our present arrangements, which first appeared in an article which I wrote for *Lloyds Bank Review* in 1955, entitled 'Notes on Public Finance':

> The position under our present tax laws of married persons with independent incomes which add up to more than a certain figure is an anomaly to which attention has frequently been drawn: they would be better off if they lived together without being married. This, of course, is a direct effect of progression; under a strictly proportionate tax, it would be a matter of indifference whether incomes were aggregated or not. It is a somewhat surprising circumstance, in a community professing respect for the institution of matrimony, that it has been tolerated for so long. For it is in fact a direct tax on marriage — to be more precise, on marriage among the rather better-off middle classes.

The Report of the Royal Commission devotes some attention to this problem. But it is perhaps questionable whether its arguments here have the force and cogency which they have in so many other directions.

The Commissioners first point out that this anomaly does not affect all married persons and that it is not until aggregate incomes reach certain levels that the tax on marriage begins. This is true, and, as a corrective of loose statements, is doubtless very much in order. But from the ethical point of view it does not seem to go very far. The tax remains a tax in the instances where it is levied; and it is surely not a very creditable feature of a tax system that it discriminates between income groups in respect of incentive or disincentive to marriage.

The Commissioners then go on to assure us that it is very doubtful whether the effect of the tax in positively encouraging what they call 'more casual associations' is in fact at all extensive. Probably this is true, though, in the nature of things, supporting evidence must have been very hard to obtain. As a people we attach great importance to the married state and we are prepared to make great sacrifices to achieve it. But it is difficult to see how the failure of a policy to produce a certain effect, because of strong resistant moral factors, can be regarded as being in itself a very convincing vindication of the moral status of that policy; we may be gratified that the citizens have not been deflected from virtue by the operation of a certain penalty, but we do not, for that reason, regard the penalty as justifiable. We may be confident that the Commissioners would have condemned in the strongest possible terms a *subsidy* to 'more casual associations'. Yet the distinction between immunity from a tax and eligibility for a positive subsidy, though real, is hardly so great as to warrant complete reprobation in the one case and comparative lack of concern in the other. Nor, from the ethical point of view, does it seem that matters are made any better by a warning that the rectification of the anomaly would be expensive to the Exchequer: the greater the expense of rectification, the greater the tax upon marriage.

It is my submission, however, that we should not be content with mere rectification by abolishing aggregation. There is an opportunity here for an innovation of policy which would give marriage and the family a place in the tax system corresponding to our continual lip-service to the national importance of these institutions. Under the American system, roughly speaking, husband and wife may aggregate their incomes and then each be taxed upon a half of the aggregate. Under the so-called 'quotient' system prevailing in some other countries this process of aggregation and division is extended to the family, with each child counting as a certain fraction of an adult for purposes of division. A system of this sort solves at one stroke, so to speak, the double problem of eliminating some of the injustice of progression and of providing allowances for children in some measure proportionate to the expenses of the income group into which they are born — a counter-agent to the differential birth rate. The fact that arrangements of this kind are actually in force elsewhere should at least give pause to any tendency to dismiss the suggestion as frivolous. Why should a nation which professes to regard the family as the essential foundation of society not do more to give recognition to that status in its system of public finance? And is there any reason to suppose that change on these lines would be opposed to popular sentiment?

# 5

## HAYEK ON LIBERTY [1]

### I

THIS is a very ambitious book. 'It has been a long time', says the author, 'since that ideal of freedom which inspired modern Western civilization and whose partial realization made possible the achievements of that civilization, was effectively restated' : [2] it is such a restatement which is here attempted. The range covered is extensive : social philosophy, jurisprudence, economics, and politics are all summoned to make their contribution to the main theme and a broad historical perspective informs the whole. In a revealing passage Professor Hayek explains that, although he still regards himself as mainly an economist, he has 'come to feel more and more that the answers to many of the pressing social questions of our time are to be found ultimately in the recognition of principles that lie outside the scope of technical economics or of any other single discipline'. [3] It is with such principles that this book is chiefly concerned.

The argument falls into three parts. The first deals with fundamentals : the nature of liberty, its value, and its relation to other notions and objectives — responsibility, employment, equality, and majority rule. The second is devoted to a conception which the author regards as quite pivotal to the constitution of liberty, namely, the rule of law, its essential characteristics, and its vicissitudes in time and place. The third, which is entitled 'Freedom in the Welfare State', consists of a series of applications of the principles thus developed to problems of contemporary policy : the place of Trade Unions in a free society, Social Security, Progressive Taxation, Housing and Town Planning, Agriculture and

[1] A review article on *The Constitution of Liberty*, by F. A. Hayek, reprinted from *Economica*, February 1961.     [2] *Ibid.* p. 1.     [3] *Ibid.* p. 3.

Conservation, Education and Research, and so on. A post-script entitled 'Why I am not a Conservative' brings the whole to a conclusion.

Let it be said at once that the result of all this is a book which certainly rises to the high plane of the matters with which it elects to deal and which, by reason both of the depth of its analysis and the width of its learning, must surely take an honourable place among the standard works on the subject. Nor is the tone less impressive than the content. The issues discussed are intrinsically controversial and the author obviously attaches great importance to his conclusions, yet the theme is set forth with studied modera-tion and the appeal is to reason rather than to emotion. It cannot be said to be easy reading; the arguments, although clear and well marshalled, demand frequent pauses for reflection. Nor is it likely, even with those who are in general sympathy with the position it adopts, to command continuous assent; considering the extraordinary difficulty of the prob-lems involved, it would be surprising if it did. But it is a book which must be taken seriously; it is not to be disposed of by guying occasional judgments. Indeed, it may be said to be a test, not of its quality but of its readers, that even where it arouses most disagreement, there at least it should command respect.

If, therefore, in what follows, the emphasis seems to dwell on points of difference, that must be taken as springing, not from any lack of warm admiration for the work as a whole, but rather as a tribute to the spirit in which it is written and a testimony to its thought-provoking power. I have written as I should talk if we were having a friendly discussion in the staff seminar here,[1] as we have done so often in the past.

## II

Professor Hayek's conception of liberty, like that of the great liberal thinkers of the past, runs in terms of absence of arbitrary coercion. In Sir Isaiah Berlin's useful classifica-

[1] That is to say The London School of Economics.

tion [1] it is the negative conception. Some coercion there must be in order to provide a sanction for the framework of law which creates the possibility of liberty. But, beyond that, it is of the essence of liberty that the individual should be free from constraint by others and that, in relation to the law, he can adjust his conduct as he does to impersonal natural limitations.

All this is excellent and has seldom been argued with greater persuasive power, especially in relation to the rival 'positive' conceptions. Professor Hayek has little difficulty in exposing the essential confusion involved in bringing under one heading the freedom involved by the absence of coercion and the so-called freedom from want which is said to flow from a certain level of real income. The limitations imposed on us by nature and technique are not the same as the limitations imposed on us by other men, and although resounding oratorical effects may be achieved by assuming that they are, yet nothing but confusion in thought and action can be the consequence. Nor is any good purpose to be served by describing liberty as a state of affairs conducive to inner freedom or to the realization of the best self; this also can open the door to all sorts of muddles and worse. It is hard enough to realize liberty in the traditional liberal sense without it being loaded with all sorts of extraneous and often contradictory associations.

Matters become more difficult, however, when political liberties are concerned. Professor Hayek would have us draw a sharp line between liberty in his sense and the right to vote; and it is not at all difficult to see why he does so. There may be much personal liberty under despotism — historically this has often been so — whereas political democracy resting on the right to vote may quite easily go totalitarian — for which there are also many historical and contemporary instances. Nevertheless, I venture to submit that not to be allowed to participate in making the law under which one has to live, to be prevented, if necessary by force, from entering the polling booth, must surely be described as

[1] See his notable Inaugural Lecture, *Two Concepts of Liberty*, Oxford, 1958.

a deprivation of liberty. The voteless citizen of mature years and understanding, however free in other respects, must be regarded in this respect as suffering a discriminatory exclusion, and if we have regard to the way in which the absence of the right to vote has resulted in other discriminatory exclusions, especially where women or coloured people have been concerned, this cannot be dismissed as a trifling matter. A full realization of liberty, in terms of Professor Hayek's general conception of absence of coercive constraint, must therefore involve the liberty to vote. That this carries with it liberty to destroy other liberty is undeniable, and we may agree with J. S. Mill and Professor Hayek that, for this reason, popular government carries with it very grave dangers. But this is just one of those paradoxes of life which are not to be eliminated by restricting the connotations of terminology.

There is a further matter in respect of which I do not feel that Professor Hayek's definitions completely catch the spirit of his general analysis. In his conception, the absence of coercion depends essentially upon the existence of known rules equally applicable to all. His discussion in this connection is one of the most impressive features of his whole argument: the case for the rule of law, divested of the misconception which marred Dicey's classic treatment, is presented with a weight of historical learning and logical force which can only be described as masterly. But is this the whole of the story? Cannot law in this sense be oppressive and restrictive? Must we not distinguish between a liberal rule of law and others?

Professor Hayek is not unaware of this question. 'It is not to be denied that even general, abstract rules, equally applicable to all, may possibly constitute severe restrictions on liberty', he says. But he goes on to minimize the difficulty. 'When we reflect on it,' he continues, 'we see how very unlikely this is. The chief safeguard is that the rules must apply to those who lay them down and those who apply them . . . and that nobody has the power to grant exception. If all that is prohibited and enjoined is prohibited and enjoined for all without exception . . . little that anybody may reasonably wish to do is likely to be prohibited.' And he urges that it is 'significant that religious beliefs seem to be almost the only ground on which general rules seriously restrictive of liberty have ever been universally enforced'.[1]

I am afraid that I do not find this very reassuring. For reasons which I do not follow, Professor Hayek seems to think that 'most such restrictions imposed on all' are 'comparatively innocuous beside those likely to be imposed on some'. This perplexes me. I am quite prepared to admit that discriminatory restriction may be more hateful than restriction which is general. But I should have thought that some of the most repellent restrictions in history had been religious; even in twentieth-century societies some of the prohibitions regarding, say, contraception and divorce, which in some countries are enforced in the name of religion, are only one degree less odious and contemptible than racial discrimination itself. Moreover, even if communism is not to be described as a religion, many of its prohibitions are generally applicable, and I should scarcely have described these as just 'irksome', the adjective which Professor Hayek uses for his own somewhat quaint example — the Scottish Sabbath.

### III

One of the most interesting sections in Professor Hayek's treatment of fundamentals is that in which, following a train of thought developed in his Dublin Lecture of 1945, *Individualism, True and False*, he distinguishes between what, in his view, are true and false theories of liberty.[2] The one, typified by the thought of the Scottish philosophers Hume, Adam Smith, and Ferguson, he describes as empirical (or occasionally anti-rationalist) : it finds the essence of freedom in spontaneity and the absence of coercion. The other, typified by the thinkers of the French Enlightenment, Rousseau, and the Physiocrats, and, somewhat surprisingly, the nineteenth-century English Utilitarians, he describes as rationalist : it believes freedom to be realized and attained

[1] *Op. cit.* pp. 154-5.  [2] *Ibid.* pp. 1-32.

only in the pursuit of an absolute collective purpose. The one conceives of reason as acting within a framework of institutions and morals, the product of more or less unconscious evolutionary experiment. The other conceives of an independent antecedent human reason that invented these institutions or at least, by a fiction, sanctioned them, and by which they can be judged as a whole. The one leads to true liberty: the other very easily turns into its opposite.

I have no doubt that much of this is very true and very important. From the positive point of view, the recognition of an order in society which has not been planned as a totality is clearly fundamental, and never has the path-breaking significance of the great eighteenth-century discoveries in this respect been better set forth than in Professor Hayek's luminous exposition, itself the source of many new insights. As he develops the conception of a spontaneous organization which is not only a sorting out of comparative aptitudes and technical advantages, but also a means of utilizing and developing a heritage of knowledge never capable of being grasped as a whole by any of the participants in the process, the time-honoured theme of the advantages of the division of labour assumes a new aspect, and propositions that have been repeated more or less parrot-wise for a hundred and fifty years acquire a meaning and depth seldom before realized. I would venture to pick this out, together with his earlier papers on similar topics, as one of Professor Hayek's most enduring contributions to our subject.[1] Nor is the negative emphasis of his analysis less relevant to the main theme. The belief that society owes its origin to rational deliberation on its shape as a whole is manifestly false. The belief that it is within the power of reason to re-shape society at one go is a dangerous delusion — the fallacy of holism against which Karl Popper has argued so powerfully. To ignore those aspects of social relationships and institutions which are the result of spontaneous adaptation rather than deliberate authoritarian contrivance is often to miss the most powerful and beneficial

[1] Reprinted in his *Individualism and Economic Order*, 1949.

elements. To initiate change without paying due heed to them is to risk failure and sometimes much worse than failure — social disaster. The difference between British and French history in this respect may perhaps be conceived as in some measure an exemplification of this danger.

Nevertheless, I have some reserves in this connection, both regarding the manner of formulation and the substance.

First, as regards manner, I must confess to a certain disquiet at finding the position to which, on the whole, I incline, described as an *anti*-rationalist position. Doubtless, if rationalism is to be conceived solely in terms of Descartes and his influence, there is good historical justification for so describing the opposition; furthermore, both in this chapter and elsewhere, Professor Hayek is careful to distinguish this 'anti-rationalist' opposition to the false use of reason from irrationalism — rejection of reason in its proper sphere. Nevertheless, I cannot help thinking that it is a term which is likely to be misunderstood and, if for that reason only, should be avoided.

Moreover — and here perhaps we approach a little nearer to substance — while I am largely in agreement with this emphasis on the importance of the non-rational element in social habits and institutions, I confess to a certain fear that, with the less sophisticated, such an emphasis may topple over into indiscriminate acceptance and admiration. After all, not all institutions and habits which survive are to be regarded as beneficial; some at least are unmitigated evils which to treat with respect were absurd. It is certainly not a 'rationalist fallacy' to subject them to critical scrutiny. In this connection, I find a very significant contrast between Hume and Burke, whom Professor Hayek tends to bracket together. Hume usually seems to me to be about right: he certainly recognizes the limitations of reason in respect to the origins of institutions and morals; yet he never hesitates to use it where it is appropriate in criticizing the extent to which they satisfy the test of public utility. Whereas Burke, for all his wisdom and insight, which no man of sense would wish ever to deny, not infrequently lets his sense of the majesty of the past degenerate into what I, at least, should regard as indefensible conservatism. It is all very well for Professor Hayek to claim him as a Whig; doubtless, even to the end, there were strong traces of that tradition. But it was not the Whig in Burke which became the bible of the European reaction and it was not the Whig which was the legitimate subject of Peacock's entertaining satire. Speaking broadly, I would say that Professor Hayek's emphasis on the spontaneous and non-rational origin of important elements in the social order is of quite fundamental importance for the liberal outlook, but that it is liable to become the foundation of an illiberal mysticism rather than 'true' liberalism unless it is understood that such elements are subject at all times to critical scrutiny from the standpoint of the requirements of public utility.

But this brings me to a much more fundamental point. I must admit that I have always found the greatest difficulty in accepting Professor Hayek's disposition to classify the nineteenth-century English Utilitarians with his 'false' Continental Rationalists, and I feel that this is apt to lend support to illiberal uses of Professor Hayek's main position. I say this with diffidence, for there are few men living from whom I have learnt so much of the history of thought as I have from Professor Hayek, and I know that his position in this respect has been held by other high authorities.[1] Nevertheless, I cannot persuade myself that it does justice to the facts : no one would seriously suggest that, for all its crudities and, if you like, errors, the thought of Bentham and the Mills *as regards epistemology* did not stand foursquare within the tradition of English empiricism — as opposed to rationalism — and I should have thought that the onus of proof must lie very heavily with those who, *as regards political philosophy*, would wrest it out of a similar place in a closely allied tradition. Moreover, I will confess unashamedly that I do not think that the main drift of nineteenth-century English Utilitarian thought tends to a liberalism which, in

[1] *E.g.*, H. J. Laski, *Political Thought in England from Locke to Bentham*, p. 21, where Rousseau and Bentham are conjoined under a common generalization.

any sense intelligible to me, deserves the appellation 'false'.[1] As the issue here is of some importance both as regards the history of thought and as regards fundamental social theory, I trust that an explicit statement of the grounds of difference will not be thought out of order.

It is not difficult to make out a case for Professor Hayek's classification. If we compare the writings of the nineteenth-century English Utilitarians with those of the eighteenth-century philosophers whom he designates as 'true' liberals or individualists, there can be no doubt that we find considerable differences, at any rate so far as Bentham and James Mill are concerned — J. S. Mill and Sidgwick [2] present a more complicated appearance, which I should have thought on balance to be less favourable to Professor Hayek's case. There are differences of style and there are differences of substance. There is a truculence and acerbity about the enunciation of fundamental principles by Jeremy Bentham, for instance, which is far removed from the tentativeness and urbanity of the formulations of David Hume. And the criticism of laws and institutions is far more radical : Hume on the whole was not discontented with things as they were, Bentham was a zealous reformer. Moreover, it has often been suggested that the calculus of utility as set forth by the Benthamites might ultimately prove an argument for collectivist rather than individualist measures, both in the sphere of public finance and in regard to the organization of production.[3] At first sight, therefore, it does not seem implausible to class Bentham and his disciples with the zealots of the French Enlightenment rather than with the calm philosophers of our middle Georgian age.

[1] In this connection, see also Sir Roy Harrod's important critique of the earlier version of Professor Hayek's classification; 'Professor Hayek on Individualism', *Economic Journal*, vol. lvi (1946), p. 435.

[2] The unsuspecting reader will, I fancy, be a trifle surprised to find the noble and temperate Sidgwick in Professor Hayek's heretics' gallery. But here he is on p. 419 where his *Elements of Politics*, although recognized to be 'in many respects an admirable work', is stigmatized as 'already strongly tainted with that rationalist utilitarianism which led to socialism'.

[3] See, for instance, Dicey, *Law and Public Opinion in England during the Nineteenth Century*, pp. 303-10.

But to do this seems to me to mistake superficialities for substance. For the critical division in social philosophy, both in the eighteenth and the nineteenth centuries, is surely between those who judge laws and institutions in terms of conformity to an abstract scheme of rights, deduced in some way or other from the principles of pure reason, and those who judge them in terms of the utility of their consequences — the judgment being, of course, in terms of rational analysis but the ultimate criterion, as both Hume and Bentham showed, being something outside reason. It is the division between those who cry 'let justice be done, if the skies fall', and those who would regard the falling of the skies to be one of the consequences which must be taken into account before it is decided whether a particular action or a particular framework of action is, or is not, just. It is the division between those who argue that the specification of a good society is something which can be set out in a few well-chosen propositions, based on 'the nature of things and of men' [1] and applicable at all times and all places, and those who argue that the conditions of life being complex and the ultimate criteria of the good being feelings rather than reasons, no such simplicity is possible.

Now, so far as this division is concerned, there can be little doubt that Bentham and those who were influenced by him are to be classified in the same group as Hume and the other eighteenth-century utilitarians, and therefore in a group opposite to Professor Hayek's 'false' rationalists. We know that, in the historical preface to the second edition of the *Fragment on Government*, Hume is singled out by Bentham himself as the source of his phrase, the principle of utility; [2]

---

[1] See, for instance, the conversation between Mercier de la Rivière and Catherine the Great quoted in my *Theory of Economic Policy in English Classical Political Economy*, p. 35.

[2] We know also the celebrated footnote to chapter 1, paragraph 36 of the same work, in which, after referring to the demonstration in the *Treatise on Human Nature* of the proposition 'that the foundations of all *virtue* are laid in *utility*', Bentham goes on: 'For my own part, I well remember, no sooner had I read that part of the work which touches on this subject, than I felt as if scales had fallen from my eyes. I then, for the first time, learnt to call the cause of the people the cause of virtue.

and, although the style and mode of exposition differ radically, both in their specific affirmations and in their rejections, the substantial identity of view between these two thinkers is remarkable. Hume found the 'sole origin' and justification of property to be public utility.[1] So did Bentham. Hume mocks gently at the concepts of 'rationalist' politics and declares that with 'the writers on the laws of nature you will always find that, whatever principles they set out with, they are sure to terminate here at last and to assign, as the ultimate reason for every rule they establish, the convenience and necessities of mankind'.[2] Bentham, embarrassed by his election as an honorary citizen of revolutionary France, declares natural rights to be nonsense, 'natural and imprescriptible rights, rhetorical nonsense — nonsense upon stilts'.[3] Why, it may be asked, is the one to be classified as a 'true' individualist, the other with the 'false' individualists whose absurdities he so drastically condemned?

Professor Hayek makes much of an allegation that 'Not Locke, nor Hume, nor Smith, nor Burke, could ever have argued as Bentham did, that every law is an evil for every law is an infraction of liberty'.[4] On this, I suggest that the appropriate comment must be that neither would Bentham — in the ultimate sense of Professor Hayek's argument, that is to say in the sense of a *net* evil. Surely it is clear that in the Benthamite calculus every law has a double aspect, the pain (evil) it inflicts by coercion and the pleasure (good) it permits by preventing other pains. Good laws are laws which result in a surplus of pleasure, bad laws a surplus of pain.[5] In the broad context of his thought, the quotation is decidedly congruous with this interpretation, but fortunately we have Bentham's own words on the subject in language so definite and so astringent as to leave little room for doubt.

[1] *Inquiry concerning the Principles of Morals: Essays Moral, Political and Literary*, Ed. Green and Grose, vol. ii, pp. 179 and 183.   [2] *Ibid.* p. 189.

[3] *Anarchical Fallacies. Works*, Ed. Bowring, vol. ii, p. 501.

[4] Hayek, *op. cit.* p. 60. The quotation from Bentham is from Hildreth's translation of *The Theory of Legislation*, 4th edition, p. 48.

[5] 'The *evil* produced is the outgo, the *good* which results is the income.' *The Theory of Legislation*, p. 32.

In the *Manual of Political Economy*, expatiating on the significance of taxation, he points out first that a tax is a sub-
traction from the pleasures of the taxed. He then goes on
to say that 'It would, however, be a gross error, and an
extremely mischievous one, to refer to the defalcation thus
resulting from the mass of liberty or free agency, as affording
a conclusive objection against the interposition of the law
for this or any other purpose', and then, broadening the
horizon of generalization, 'Every law which does not consist
in the repeal or partial repeal of a coercive law, is itself a
coercive law. To reprobate as a mischief resulting from
that law, a property which is the essence of all law, is to
betray a degree of ignorance one should hardly think
possible on the part of a mind accustomed to the contem-
plation of any branch of the system of the laws — a total
unacquaintance with what may be called the logic of the
laws.'[1] It is difficult to believe that Locke, or Hume, or
Smith, or Burke would have disagreed with this.

It might be argued, I suppose, that the Greatest Happiness Principle which figures so prominently in the Benthamite
façade, is just another formula on all fours with the fundamental declarations inspired by the 'rationalist' outlook.
But this would be a misapprehension. The 'rationalist'
declarations claimed definite status as the foundations of
social order. *They were ultimate solutions* — 'all you know on
earth and all you need to know'. The Utilitarian formula,
by contrast, offered simply *a criterion by which particular
solutions could be judged*. The one offered a simple list of
rights and duties applicable to all societies : the other a
principle by which the detailed prescriptions of particular
codes and systems of law might be put to a general test. It
is perhaps arguable — though, in my judgment, the thing
has been somewhat overdone [2] — that Bentham himself did

---

[1] *Works*, Ed. Bowring, vol. iii, p. 34.
[2] Largely as a result of the picture painted by J. S. Mill at the time of his
maximum reaction from Benthamism. But Mill did not know Bentham until
Bentham was a very old man, and there is good reason to suppose that in all
sorts of ways he subtly misconceived the master. See Everett, *The Education of
Jeremy Bentham, passim.*

not pay enough attention to the lessons of history. But any suggestion that it was ever believed by him that the adoption of his principle would automatically churn out a code which was universally valid regardless of local or historical differences, cannot survive even the most cursory inspection of the *Essay on the Influence of Time and Place in Matters of Legislation*.[1]

Moreover, it is getting things very much out of proportion to think of Bentham as primarily concerned with the elaboration of a general formula. His major achievement, the achievement which entitles him to rank among the great thinkers and benefactors of mankind, was in the sphere of applications. And his method — which J. S. Mill happily named 'the method of detail',[2] the method, namely, of treating wholes by splitting them up into parts — was the main characteristic of his work. In practice, the famous calculus served chiefly as a rough reminder that, when judging particular laws and institutions, it is necessary to take into account their influence, positive and negative, on *all* the individuals likely to be affected. It is hardly possible to think of a contrast more complete than the contrast between the exhibitionist rhetoric of a Rousseau and the painstaking examination of detail of a Bentham.[3]

As for the extreme radicalism of Bentham's approach, particularly in his later years — his antipathy to Blackstone, his jeers at the 'Matchless Constitution' — here, no doubt, we have an attitude which may well be thought to be, in

---

[1] *Works*, Ed. Bowring, vol. i, pp. 170-94.

[2] J. S. Mill, *Dissertations and Discussions*, vol. i, pp. 339-40.

[3] In this connection it may be of interest to quote Bentham's own comment on the contrast. 'The first business, according to the plan I am combatting', he argues, 'is to find and declare the principles, the laws of a fundamental nature; that done, it is by their means that we shall be enabled to find the proper laws of detail. I say no: it is only in proportion as we have found and compared with one another the laws of detail, that our fundamental laws will be exact and fit for service. . . . What is the source of this premature anxiety to establish fundamental laws. It is the old conceit of being wiser than posterity — wiser than those who will have had more experience.' *Anarchical Fallacies. Works*, Ed. Bowring, vol. iii, p. 494. I should have thought that this last comment would have been especially congenial to Professor Hayek; for what is it but an application to the future, of his own justification of the evolution of law in the past?

some respects at least, the exact opposite of Burke's. But it is not for that reason to be classified as untrue to the spirit of liberalism. For on this matter the verdict of history is clearly on Bentham's side. The legal and institutional abuses which were the target of his criticism were real abuses. The reforms which flowed from his efforts and those of his followers were lasting improvements. Why then should we describe as a 'false' liberalism the critical analysis and the constructive imagination on which they were based? Indeed, I will confess that, from my point of view, if this were falsity, the 'true' liberalism of some of their predecessors, including Hume, could have benefited by a slight infusion. If any unsophisticated reader, carried away by the cogency and authority of Professor Hayek's argument, is led to think of Benthamism in its main historical aspects as something which is to be bracketed with the pseudo-logic of the more Messianic social creeds, let him read some cold description of pre-Bentham legal proceedings and institutions in the United Kingdom. Let us hope that the shock he will get will not lead him into the opposite error of imagining that all reforms are possible overnight and that it only needs a little ingenuity to purge the system of all anomalies without harm to anyone or anything. But at least he will see another aspect of the subject which demands due consideration.[1]

There remains only the tendency to collectivism alleged to be implicit in the Greatest Happiness Principle. Now

[1] Professor Hayek must forgive me if, in this connection, I contrast his attitude with that of Acton whom he admires so much. According to Professor Hayek, 'Bentham and his Utilitarians did much to destroy the beliefs which England had in part preserved from the Middle Ages, by their scornful treatment of most of what until then had been the most admired feature of the British constitution'. And (this, incidentally, well illustrates Professor Hayek's peculiar pejorative use of the word 'rational'), 'they introduced into Britain what had so far been entirely absent — the desire to remake the whole of her law and institutions on rational lines . . .' (p. 174). According to Acton: 'A century ago it was well known that whoever had an audience of a Master in Chancery was made to pay for three, but no man heeded the enormity until it suggested to a young lawyer that it might be well to question and examine with rigorous suspicion every part of the system in which such things were done. The day on which that gleam lighted up the clear hard mind of Jeremy Bentham is memorable in the political calendar beyond the entire administration of many statesmen.' (*The History of Freedom and other Essays* by John Emerich Edward Dalberg-Acton, First Baron Acton, p. 3.)

there can clearly be no denying that some utilitarians, from William Thompson onwards, have been thoroughgoing collectivists — though, I suspect, they have been the exceptions rather than the rule — and attempts have often been made to justify some collectivist measures by appeal to utilitarian principle. But it seems hard to blame all this on Bentham and his friends. If Professor Hayek is thinking of progressive taxation, he will find the pseudo-law of diminishing social utility clearly adumbrated in an *obiter dictum* of Hume,[1] and some justification for the progressive principle itself in Adam Smith's remarks on the taxation of houses [2] — whereas an indictment almost as severe as his own is to be found in J. S. Mill's *Principles*.[3] As for the main principle of economic organization, can there really be much doubt that Bentham was in the main an individualist? I should have thought that his repeated insistence, even against Adam Smith,[4] that adult individuals were the best judges of what knowledge was relevant to their immediate action, would have been specially acceptable to anyone stressing, as does Professor Hayek, the importance of the division of labour in this respect. And even though J. S. Mill, as is notorious, was willing to regard himself as a socialist as regards small-scale experiments in co-operative ownership and organization, it must always be remembered — what is nearly always forgotten — that nowhere in the literature is there a more tremendous warning of the evils of overall collectivization

[1] *Op. cit.* p. 188 : 'It must be confessed that whenever we depart from this equality we rob the poor of more satisfaction than we add to the rich.'

[2] It is not very unreasonable that the rich should contribute to the public expense, not only in proportion to their revenue, but something more than a proportion.' *Wealth of Nations*, Ed. Cannan, vol. ii, p. 327.

[3] *Principles*, Ed. Ashley, p. 808.

[4] See especially *The Defence of Usury*, Letter XIII, *passim*. (*Works*, Ed. Bowring, vol. iii, pp. 20-9), especially the following which I should have thought to be almost quintessential Hayek. 'Is it endurable that the legislator should by violence substitute his own pretended reason, the result of a momentary and scornful glance, the offspring of wantonness and arrogance, much rather than social anxiety and study, in the place of the humble reason of individuals, binding itself down with all its force to that very object which he pretends to have in view? Nor let it be forgotten, that on the side of the individual in this strange competition, there is the most perfect and minute knowledge and information which interest, the whole interest of a man's reputation and fortune can engender; on the side of the legislator, the most perfect ignorance.'

than in the well-known passage in *Liberty*.[1]   It is true that
Bentham and his followers were not doctrinaire individualists,
in, say, the manner of Herbert Spencer.   They recognized
that there were conditions of society when economic paternalism was justifiable.   They recognized too that there were
cases where, external economies or diseconomies being conspicuous, some form of collectivist control was sanctioned by
the test of utility, and not believing themselves to be in
complete possession of all relevant social knowledge, they
were not opposed to all experiments in collectivist organization.   But in this, surely, they were only talking good sense
and good economic analysis.   I see no reason whatever why,
for these reasons, the most devoted believer in liberty should
deny them the title of 'true' individualists or force upon
them classification with Cartesian rationalists.[2]

IV

The final section of Professor Hayek's book is entitled
'Freedom in the Welfare State'.   I am inclined slightly to
regret this title since I doubt the expediency of bringing all
the subjects discussed under this kind of blanket classification.
I suppose that the words 'Welfare State' do stand for something which, in contrast to the picture of an earlier age,
does have some kind of meaning.   But, as the contents of
this section themselves show, as soon as we come to look at
what are regarded as characteristic features we find that, to

---

[1] See above p. 39.

[2] Professor Hayek very rightly lays emphasis upon the Cartesian influences
on his 'false' individualism.   I cannot help wondering whether in deciding
to put Bentham among the Cartesians, he did not perhaps forget what Jeremy
himself had to say about the philosopher in question and his habits of thought.
Appropriately enough it occurs in the analysis of Article I of the Declaration
of Rights.   '*Whatever is, is* — was the maxim of Descartes, who looked upon it
as so sure, as well as so instructive a truth, that everything else which goes by
the name of truth might be deduced from it.   The philosophical vortex-maker
— *who, however mistaken in his philosophy and his logic* (my italics) was harmless
enough at least little thought how soon a part of his own countrymen, fraught
with pretensions as empty as his own, and as mischievous as his were innocent,
would contest with him even this his favourite and fundamental maxim by
which everything else was to be brought to light. . . .' *Anarchical Fallacies*.
*Works*, Ed. Bowring, vol. iii, p. 499.

discuss them intelligently, they have to be split up and treated separately. Thus, for instance, the problem whether special legal privileges for trade unions are or are not desirable from the liberal point of view is something which is skies apart from the problems of state-aided education. True that in a formal textbook of the old-fashioned type they would both perhaps figure in the section on the functions of the state. But, so far as I can see, that is about all.

I submit that this is something more than a mere verbal quibble. For it seems to me that much confusion is caused by argument in terms of such vague hold-all descriptions. The question, 'Are you, or are you not, in favour of the Welfare State?' is, in my conception, the sort of question to which a reasonable man should refuse a simple answer. For, surely, from almost any conceivable point of view, the answer must be that one approves of some things and disapproves of others. Yet discussion is frequently posed on this plane, both by those who expect a favourable reply and those who expect the reverse. And I cannot help feeling that Professor Hayek, who will be suspected by at least half his reviewers of being 'against' the Welfare State, runs the danger by his choice of title of having his detailed arguments discussed, not in terms of their merits, but rather in terms of some equally wide (and misleading) description of their tendency as a whole. And that, I think will be a very great pity. For, whether you agree with him or not on the various subjects under consideration, he has always something to say which deserves respectful consideration.

At the outset let it be said that this is by no means always negative. It is true that there is vigorous criticism, some of it of very great force: I personally should find it impossible to refute the main criticisms of special privileges for associations of producers, trade unions, or otherwise; the exposure of the crass inequity and diseconomy of rent restriction, one of the meanest of all demagogic expedients, seems to me quite unanswerable; and I think that there is much more in the strictures on progressive taxation, at any rate extreme progression, than many of the critics will concede. But, as befits one who derives so much from the great traditions of English Political Economy — not only of the eighteenth century but also of the nineteenth — Professor Hayek's attitude is not one of *laissez-faire* in the sense of leaving nothing to government but the functions of the night watchman. Side by side with his critique of *étatiste* policies, there are developed a series of alternatives which, set out in a more systematic form, might well be regarded as liberal agenda for state action. Thus, for instance, following J. S. Mill, he states powerfully the case for compulsory education and, with various reserves — some of which I find difficult to follow — he favours some state assistance for those who are unable to afford it. But, again following J. S. Mill, whose grave warning is the motto of his chapter,[1] he sees serious dangers in an exclusive provision of educational services by the state, and he gives positive blessing to the proposal which has been put forward by Milton Friedman and others [2] that parents should be given vouchers covering the costs of education, which they could then hand over to schools of their choice. Opinions may well differ, even among liberal thinkers, concerning the value or the practicability of particular items of the Hayek agenda, and it is very easy to think of directions in which they might be extended. But, cumulatively, they form a programme which those who have the cause of individual freedom at heart could do well to ponder seriously.

Having said this, however, I should be highly disingenuous if I were to conceal the fact that there are aspects of Professor Hayek's approach in some of these connections about which I have very considerable hesitation : I find some of his treatment one-sided, and I doubt very much the justification of some of his more extreme apprehensions.

---

[1] 'A general state education is a mere contrivance for moulding people to be exactly like one another, and the mould in which it casts them is that which pleases the predominant power in the government, whether this be a monarch, a priesthood, an aristocracy or the majority of the existing generation.' *On Liberty*, p. 95.

[2] See, for instance, the interesting article by Mr. Wiseman in the *Scottish Journal of Political Economy*, vol. vi, pp. 48-58.

I can illustrate both these kinds of difficulty from his discussion of the problems of social security. On these he has some things to say which seem to me both true and important. I find very impressive his plea that a part, at least, of the deductions from earnings which now form so conspicuous a feature of certain social security systems of Western Europe might well have been left in the hands of the earners to invest in private insurance policies more adapted to their own conceptions of need; and I have an instinctive sympathy with his dislike of centralized systems which in the nature of things cannot develop more than a limited degree of flexibility and, in the absence of continual vigilance, are liable to considerable abuses. I see much to be said for the view, so powerfully developed by Mr. Hagenbuch,[1] that if our hope is that the members of the poorer classes shall eventually enjoy the present standards of the middle class, it is desirable to frame our institutions so as to allow the development of middle-class habits of independence, and I am inclined to believe that some of our present practices in regard to social security may tend in the other direction.

But I cannot regard all that has happened with the degree of disquiet which it so obviously arouses in Professor Hayek; if I think of the system I know best, that of the United Kingdom, my reaction is much more mixed. I agree that the weight of our taxation is an embarrassment — though I am far from thinking, as I suspect Professor Hayek does, that we are in a state of economic decline. I agree too that the degree of progression where the higher incomes are concerned is both unfair and unwise. But it is surely a great mistake to blame all this on our social legislation. Whether the conceptions be good or bad, I should have thought that they could be easily afforded, were it not for the magnitude of our expenditure on defence; and while, in the present international situation, I have no desire to see that cut, it seems to me that to lay all the blame on the social services for any resulting complications, is to get things quite out of

[1] *Lloyds Bank Review*, July 1953, pp. 1-16.

proportion. Similarly, with extreme progression — the contribution made here to substantial redistribution is small. The social security system and social services in general could go on more or less as at present, even if a Chancellor of the Exchequer should pluck up enough courage to decree that no one should be taxed more than, say, three-fifths of his marginal income.

Moreover, there is a positive side, which I should have thought, on any calm assessment of the position, needs bringing into the picture. It may very well be that some liberties have been curtailed which we should wish to retain and that some habits have been fostered which we should wish to discourage. But I cannot believe, even on a very long-run assessment of values, that, in what is perhaps a blundering way, we have not achieved considerable positive good. I confess that, when I look at social conditions in contemporary Britain, with its well-fed, healthy, and essentially decent and humane citizens and their children, and draw the contrast with what, as a young man, I knew forty years ago, I do perceive a most solid and substantial improvement. Much of this, the greater part doubtless, is due to the growth of wealth — the product of the despised system of free enterprise. But I do not think it can reasonably be denied that some of it is due to what has been done through the state in the sphere of social services, ill-conceived as some of the mechanisms and some of the benefits may be urged to be. And when I look to all the difficult and anxious problems to come, I suspect that although we have scrambled some eggs which we may find it hard to unscramble, yet the improvement which has been achieved is not just something improvidently snatched from the future, but something which, on balance, will make it easier to go forward as a reasonably harmonious community.

But this brings me to my second scruple in this connection. I cannot suppress the conviction that Professor Hayek is somewhat too apt to extrapolate his apprehensions of evil and to assume that deviations from his norm lead cumulatively to disaster. I say this with reserve for I think that some of the criticisms which were made on this score of his *Road to Serfdom* were both ill informed and unfair; there certainly have been tendencies in history which have led to catastrophe, and those who judged his analysis of the influences leading to the growth of national socialism on the continent in terms of the evolution of Anglo-Saxon institutions exhibited an outlook which was definitely parochial, if it was not actively malicious. What worries me is not the contention that this sort of thing *may* happen but rather any assumption that it almost certainly *must*. For instance, in my judgment Professor Hayek is justifiably critical of some contemporary arrangements regarding old age pensions and apprehensive of the difficulties which may arise should the burden be greatly increased. But why should he argue as if these were at all likely to lead us to social disintegration and the concentration camp? This seems to me to be one of the less probable outcomes of the evolution of our institutions in this respect. There are some interventions, such as attempts at individual price-fixing in wartime, of which a tendency to spread may be fairly confidently predicted. There are others, such as some kinds of taxes and subsidies, or some experiments in government ownership and control where, the casual mechanisms involved being much more complicated and indirect, no such predictions are safe. And, in general, I am bound to say that, whatever may be the case in particular instances, any absolute scepticism regarding the stability of all mixed economies seems to me to have little basis in either logic or history.

The fact is, I suspect, that, when it is a question of diagnosing what we believe to be present evils, we economists are particularly liable to the temptation to drive home our points by warnings which go considerably further than the circumstances of the case would in fact justify. The appendix to Sir John Sinclair's *History of the Public Revenue* (Third Edition, 1803) contains a most salutary list of unfulfilled predictions of imminent catastrophe by English economists; and it would be very easy indeed to bring it up to date. The moral of this, of course, is not that we should sit back and say nothing or pursue only the more unreal problems of pure theory — it is very arguable that the fact that we have avoided disaster so far and done pretty well on the whole is partly due to the willingness of so many people to stick their necks out and utter warnings. It is rather that, rejecting, as we do in others, historicism with its bogus apparatus of inevitable trends and improbable cycles, we are under a special obligation to see that we do not fall into the same error ourselves when we have a case to argue. I am very conscious that I have sometimes done this myself. And I should be lacking in candour if I did not say that I think that on occasion the very strong arguments of this most sincere and important book are weakened by such a tendency.

v

This review is already too long. But I should be sorry to bring it to a close without emphasizing once more that any criticisms which I have felt impelled to make, must not be interpreted as detracting from the liveliest appreciation of the qualities of this book as a whole. It is a work which surely no one with even a bare minimum of magnanimity and sense of what is fine can read without gratitude and admiration — gratitude for a splendid contribution to the great debate, admiration for the moral ardour and intellectual power which inspired it and made it possible.

# 6

## THE MEANING OF
## ECONOMIC INTEGRATION [1]

### I

I HAD better begin by making clear the intentions and limitations of this lecture. The subject which has been assigned to me is The Meaning of Economic Integration, and I intend to discuss this in terms of the widest possible generality. I shall try to explain to you how I define economic integration and what measures I regard as necessary to bring it about. The discussion, therefore, is a discussion of a general conception: it is not a discussion of a particular project. In framing my observations, I shall naturally endeavour to keep an eye on their possible practical applications. The background of my thought is constituted by the possibilities of integration on this, the so-called Western part of the planet, at this point in the twentieth century, rather than integration on Mars or Saturn, at some indeterminate period. But the actual treatment will be theoretical. I shall try to stand back from the contemporary picture and to discern general principles rather than particular instances.

### II

Let me start by setting forth in a broad way how I conceive my subject. The term 'economic integration' as used in everyday political discussion is extremely vague. It means different things to different men — it is not difficult to perceive the political advantages of a certain penumbra of ambiguity. But, from my point of view, what I mean when I speak of integration, is perhaps well symbolized by

[1] A lecture given at the School of Advanced International Studies of the Johns Hopkins University at Bologna in the spring of 1958.

the notices on the sleeping-cars which strike my eye when I board my train at Calais to come here to give this lecture : Calais–Roma, Calais–Wien, Calais–Hamburg — what could be more civilized and sensible than unimpeded traction for men and goods from one end of Western Europe to the other ?

But, then, along come the officials at the frontiers, the passport control, the foreign exchange control, the inspectors of customs, and one wakes up to the realities of the present situation. Limitations of trade, migration, financial transfer — my ideal economic integration would sweep all that away. Much of what I have to say in this lecture will be concerned with the implications of this.

There is, however, a very different conception. Many people when they hear the term 'economic integration' think at once of smoke-filled rooms, with little knots of representatives of the different sovereign states planning the total layout of economic life in the integrating areas : so much of this kind of timber from $X$, so much from $Y$, and so on, down the whole list of raw materials ; so much to $X$, so much to $Y$, and so on, down the whole list of articles of consumption. And so with the distribution of investment and the labour force. . . .

This conception is quite different from mine. I am not attracted by the picture. I do not think that the state of affairs which it stands for, harmonizes well with our western conceptions of the requirements of a free society; and, in any case, so long as we are dealing with the integration of economic life between the inhabitants of different sovereign states, I am very doubtful indeed whether it is a very realistic conception. I think the experience of the Organization for European Economic Co-operation is fairly conclusive evidence of the impracticability of integration on these lines. It is easy enough to conceive *partial* plans of this sort — plans for the regulation of production and distribution of one or two particular commodities — which do not put a great strain on the mechanism for the co-operation between two constituent states. But *total* planning of this sort involves such a complete supersession of autonomy of the constituent states that it bursts, so to speak, the conception of voluntary co-operation. In order that it may be possible, nothing less than a total unification of political authority is necessary. Not even federation, which is something more ambitious than what I am discussing here, would be an adequate political framework. The economics of a total collectivist world state are very interesting, but they are quite definitely not my subject to-day.

In general, I submit that, when people discuss economic integration, they certainly do not exclude positive action on the part of the integrating states, but in the main they conceive that action to be directed to bringing it about that the economic relations *across* national boundaries become more like economic relations *within* national boundaries. They mean that economic life within the areas concerned becomes more interdependent, less cut off by political accident. At the same time, their ideas usually relate to the integration of a limited area. The old free traders used to speak of the eventual economic unity under free trade of the entire world. But modern talk of economic integration usually involves something considerably less comprehensive than that : the integration of Western Europe, the integration of the British Commonwealth, and so on.

This, at any rate, is what I propose to discuss this morning. I shall ask what are the implications, and what are the minimum requirements, of integration in this sense in regard to (i) trade, (ii) migration, (iii) money and monetary systems, and (iv) public finance. Then, finally, I shall enquire into the probabilities of integration on these lines : I shall reflect a little on the question whether integration is possible in the economic sphere without something approaching federation in the political sphere.

### III

Let me begin with trade ; and first of all, let me dispose of a misapprehension.

It is often argued as if the case for the integration of

trade within a limited area is the same as the case for the integration of trade throughout the world as a whole; that is to say, that the case for a customs union is the same as the case for universal free trade. But this is not true, at any rate if you are thinking of matters from the world point of view. On a certain plane of argument the case for free trade all round is a case which may be agreed — all sorts of political assumptions are involved here and the general case is subject to many qualifications and exceptions; but on this plane of argument these details can be neglected. The case for customs unions, however, that is the case for *limited* free trade, is not so unequivocal, at any rate from the world point of view.

Why is this? The essential point can be put in this way. In judging a general lowering of barriers to trade, the general effects are all that need be considered, at any rate in the first approximation. It is clear that, in the very short period, there would be both gains and losses to take into account. But in the long run, on the criteria which it is customary to adopt when judging trade policy, the gains should preponderate. In judging the effects of customs unions, however, even in the long run, there are two sets of effects to be considered: effects within the area and effects on the world outside.

Now we may assume, for purposes of argument, that, *within* the area, the integration has a clear balance of advantage — there will be more to be said about that in a moment. But, *outside* the area, there may be gain or loss. If we adopt Jacob Viner's useful terminology we can speak of trade-creating effects of such unions and trade-diverting effects; and there is no guarantee that, from the world point of view, the trade-diverting effects may not be the more important. This probably sounds abstract; and, in any rigorous statement, a host of assumptions and qualifications would be essential. But it is quite easy to think of a practical example. Suppose the formation of a customs union fosters high-cost agriculture within the area, to the exclusion of low-cost agricultural products from elsewhere.

It may be that, within the area, the sacrifice of agricultural cheapness is compensated by other gains. But from the point of view of the world at large, the consolidation and intensification of an uneconomic division of labour may mean something which must be regarded as a loss.

These considerations are reinforced if it is recollected that customs unions themselves involve obstacles to trade — tariff protection, etc. Theoretically, trade diversion of a damaging nature from the world point of view, is possible, even if the tariffs of the customs union are low; but if they are high, it is much more likely. Hence, from the world point of view, there is no *a priori* reason to regard all customs unions as good. I am inclined to guess that there are sound practical reasons for assuming a certain degree of harmony between world and special interests when fairly large areas are integrated behind fairly low customs barriers. But this is just a preliminary hunch. For accurate judgment each case would have to be considered on its merits.

Now let us confine our attention to effects within the integrating area, and to make the analysis easier, let us assume that integration is achieved without raising surrounding tariffs. What are the advantages?

As I see the picture, the advantages are of three kinds:

(*a*) First, integration makes possible a better division of labour within the area. To understand this thoroughly it has to be conceived in a large way, dynamically as well as statically. The statical gains are gains of the kind which are made comprehensible to us by the Classical Theory of Comparative Costs. This theory reveals the nature of the gains which may accrue from reallocation at constant costs of given resources — you all know the traditional arithmetical examples; it is useful, I think, to conceive these as illustrations of one aspect of the advantages of a better international division of labour.

But the wider division of labour which is made possible by economic integration involves diminishing costs; and here we encounter more dynamic consideration. The division of labour notoriously depends on the extent of the market : with greater markets there can be greater sub-division of productive processes, and the advantages here can be very great indeed. It is possible to doubt the superior efficiency of large establishments. But it is not, I think, possible to doubt the superior efficiency of large production. Imagine what would be lost if the forty-eight states of the great American union each attempted economic self-sufficiency.

(*b*) Secondly, there are advantages which accrue in the sphere of accumulation. The increased production which is due to increased division of labour, permits additional accumulation. The diminished barriers to trade permit a more effective mobilization and distribution of saving. Much, of course, depends upon a successful solution of the problems of monetary equilibrium, of which there will be something to say later. But of the potential gains in this connection there is really little room for scepticism.

(*c*) Thirdly, there are advantages from increased competition. This has two aspects, negative and positive. Negatively we know that, the wider the market, the less the opportunity for monopoly and restriction ; and that in itself is very important. But, beyond this, there is the positive gain springing from the spur to efficiency and technical progress, which derives from competition between a multiplicity of sources of supply. Personally, I set great store by this. What are the reasons for the efficiency of the U.S. economy ? A comprehensive answer would be very complicated ; all sorts of geographical and sociological factors are involved. But in the final analysis, I suspect, a great deal is due to the effects of nation-wide competition.

Such are the main advantages. It is probably worth emphasizing that the first group is almost equally conceivable whether the prevailing system of industrial organization be collectivist or individualist. The argument for extensive territorial division of labour is essentially an argument for a rational layout, a sensible disposition of resources. Your individualist thinks that this will come about through the spontaneous operation of competition and the market. The collectivist thinks that conscious control from the centre is better calculated to achieve good results. But each wishes for arrangements which, other things being equal, maximize the volume of production measured in price terms, and the argument for greater territorial division of labour is that it tends to bring this about. Neither under individualism nor under collectivism is it a sensible policy to produce at home what you can procure with less sacrifice from elsewhere by way of exchange.

But it is important not to overstate the case. It is certainly to be expected that, on balance, the increased territorial division of labour within the integrating area will make possible a larger volume of production within the area. It does not follow, however, that all productive groups necessarily participate in this gain unless there is complete mobility of labour. The old theory of comparative cost showed that there was a necessary long-run advantage for the members of *two* groups, arranging one with the other to divide their labour according to cost differentials. It did not show that, if either one sold a competing product *in a third market*, a reduction of trade barriers between them and this third market necessarily improved the position of both. This is a point which was often overlooked by the more enthusiastic advocates of free trade all round. But in fact it is pure common sense. If a particular group of producers has enjoyed more or less exclusive privileges in a limited market, there is nothing in general economic theory which would lead you to expect that they could necessarily retain these privileges, if the barriers surrounding the exclusive market were broken down and competition from elsewhere were allowed.

Hence I believe that the advocates of economic integration do well to state their arguments in terms of the probable gains *given sufficient mobility and adaptability*. They ought not to claim that there is inevitable gain for all and sundry, regardless of whether they are prepared to adapt their arrangements to the new situation. And, in any concrete case of integration, I should expect that there would emerge the possibilities of severe distress for particular groups of producers, if arrangements were not made to promote their transfer into other lines of occupation or other areas and if, while this transfer were taking place, there were not transitional arrangements to ease the difficulties of adjustment. On the other hand, provided that such arrangements exist, I should have little hesitation in saying that, at any rate within the integrating area, the general benefits arising from a better division of labour are likely considerably to outweigh its disadvantages.

What then are the minimum conditions of obtaining such advantages?

I am pretty clear that the optimal arrangement is that which prevails under federation, such as you have in the United States, namely, free movement of goods between the different states concerned. Many as are the exceptions to the presumption in favour of complete *laissez-faire* in the organization of industry, I find it extremely difficult to believe that limitation of interstate commerce is the best way of looking after them. If it is desirable, for instance, to foster an infant industry in a particular locality, then subsidies for a limited period are much better than permanent obstacles to competing imports. I confess that I find quite amazing the frame of mind which is prepared to regard the makeshift protectionist expedients of sovereign states of obviously inappropriate size, as producing a better approximation to an ideal allocation or resources than would be brought about under interstate freedom of commerce.

But I am not asking here what are the best possible arrangements. I am asking rather what are the *minimum* conditions which permit the use of the word integration in the sense in which I am using it, and I would formulate these in this way. I would not argue that complete freedom is necessary; you can imagine something which could be regarded as an approach to integration taking the form of a standstill of obstacles at a given level, although I should be reluctant to describe it this way if the obstacles were very high. I would not argue even that it is necessary that there should never be a rise in interstate obstacles. But I would argue that it is necessary that *the regulation of whatever obstacles persist should be a matter of agreement*. I would argue that it is essential to the idea of integration that, if the authorities in one part of the system wish to raise obstacles and to limit trade, this must be done by common consent. Otherwise the word integration is inappropriate. That is to say, in the last resort, the requirement of integration is not complete freedom from regulation, but rather complete agreement as to the form that regulation should take.

Whether such a halfway house as this is easier to inhabit than the more thorough-going federal arrangements under which the local authorities completely surrender their right of inter-local regulation is, of course, a question to be debated. For the moment I am content to leave it open.

## IV

I turn now to the implications of integration as regards migration. Let me say at once that I attach much more than mere economic advantage to this particular conception. Free movement, in my system of thought, is a sign of civilization. When I was young, you could still go to Victoria Station and take a ticket for anywhere in Europe west of the Russian frontier,[1] and proceed to your destination without a passport. To me it is a terrible sign of the retrogression of civilized standards that, at the present day, the majority of people seem to regard the apparatus of passports and migration control as part of the order of nature. I can think of few things that would more happily signalize the spiritual integration of the West than the suppression of this apparatus of barbarism.

But putting that on one side, the economic advantages

[1] Russian habits in this respect evidently go back a long way. According to Voltaire, 'An old law, held sacred among them, forbade them, on pain of death, to leave their own country without permission of their Patriarch. Yet this law, avowedly enacted to prevent them from realizing their state of bondage, was agreeable to a people who, in the depths of their ignorance and misery, disdained all commerce with foreign nations.' *History of Charles XII*, Everyman edition, p. 22.

are obviously very considerable. The theory of comparative costs suggests advantages in division of labour, even if migration is impossible. Marginal productivity analysis shows the advantages which may accrue if it is free. If there are no barriers to movement, it is possible for the different kinds of labour to be employed at points of equimarginal return; and this means that, in such conditions, the wealth potential is greater than would otherwise be the case.

The question may be asked, however, is not such freedom of movement associated with great economic disturbance and damage to higher income groups? The theoretical possibility may be conceded, and it may be conceded that occasionally in practice there have been upsets of this sort — the classic case, of course, is the prolongation of the misery of the English handloom weavers by continuous immigration from Ireland. But, in general, I doubt if this sort of thing is very likely. Migration does not happen all at once. Movement into an area on a large scale usually takes some time, and the groups affected have an opportunity to adapt themselves to the new situation. Moreover, it must be remembered that labour from low income areas is very often complementary to the labour in high income areas. The idea that it is necessarily competitive is not true.

It is sometimes argued, however, that even if the effects of immigration from lower to higher income areas are not economically damaging, they are liable to cause very great sociological upset. The arrival of people with different consumption patterns and a different willingness to work is said to breed enmity and misunderstanding. I have not much sympathy with this kind of argument which tends to assume that low-brow incomprehension and envy must always be in the ascendant. Nor do I think that it is borne out in practice. A good deal of movement of this sort has actually taken place without begetting the more contemptible types of social friction. The possibility, however, is not to be excluded. There is so much race and colour prejudice prevalent in this deplorable century that we cannot be sure that movements of this sort would not from time to time give rise to this kind of trouble. But if it does, I would argue that that is a case, not for absolute prohibition of movement, but rather for some degree of regulation, of which I will have more to say later.

Meanwhile, we may note that there is a much better argument for limitation of movement, namely, the argument which is based on the assumption of differences of demographic tendencies. If the inhabitants of a certain area are so fixed in habits of rapid multiplication that there is no hope of speedy change, then it is obviously in the interests of the world as a whole that they should be confined to a smaller rather than a larger area. This is not a selfish argument. It is an argument which was elaborated by so disinterested and so cosmopolitan a thinker as Edwin Cannan,[1] and, granted the assumption on which it is based, I see no valid answer to it. The dismissal of all apprehensions of world overpopulation, on the ground that 'God will provide', seems to me at once an insult to whatever deity is assumed and to the intelligence of whoever is involved in the argument.

But nevertheless the assumptions are very severe. It says that there is justification for confining certain people to the areas which they inhabit at present *if* their present habits of multiplication are deeply rooted; *if*, that is to say, there are no signs of effective diminution in the size of the average family so that a tendency to overpopulation persists. I have some fear that this assumption is fairly reasonable as regards some low-income groups from Asia and Africa. But I doubt very much whether it applies with very much force to any of the groups liable to be affected by integration movements in Western Europe or the Atlantic Community.

Again let us enquire concerning the minimum requirements of integration in this connection.

As I have said, I attach enormous importance to the eventual achievement of complete freedom of movement within the integrating area. But, in the last analysis, I am prepared to admit that it is not absolutely essential. What is essential is that any regulation which takes place should

[1] *Wealth*, Third edition, p. 287.

be based upon agreement by all the parties concerned. That is to say, that, if there are limitations of movement, there must be no scope for the complaint that they are due simply to the exclusiveness of one set of members of the integrating area.

v

I turn next to money. Before integration takes place there are different moneys in circulation within the different states. There are different central banks — that is to say, different centres of money supply in the widest sense of the word.

Now we know that, if the different moneys consisted solely of coins manufactured from a common metal and these coins were freely meltable and exportable, the fact that they bore different names and had different weights would involve no serious disunity in the monetary phenomena of the combined areas. And even where there are advanced credit systems, if their management is conducted solely with regard to the movements of the metallic reserves, not much disunity is likely to arise from the existence of different centres of organization in the different areas.

But when, as now, you have different centres of money supply and when the local policies in this respect are not focused on this single objective, then there is no necessary harmony between monetary phenomena in the different areas; and it is quite possible for difficulties on a large scale to emerge in connection with the balance of payments. They may emerge because of different rates of increase of the money supply in the different areas. They may emerge because of a refusal on the part of a particular centre to adapt its internal circulation to changing external circumstances, either favourable or unfavourable.[1] And when this happens, then there are liable to develop further disintegrating influences — quantitative restriction of trade, exchange control, and so on.

[1] For a more extensive development of this part of the argument see my *Economist in the Twentieth Century*, chapter v, *passim*.

Such troubles, as we know, have been very common in the post-war world. But it is quite conceivable that deliberate attempts at integration of other economic arrangements may, at any rate in its first stages, cause them to be even more frequent. The changes in the channels of trade, due to integration, may give rise to changes in the flows of inter-local expenditure. In the absence of a common policy or a common currency, there may occur crises on the markets for foreign exchange which otherwise would not have taken place.

For this reason some authorities have suggested that the adoption of integrated arrangements regarding trade should be accompanied by the adoption of floating rates of exchange between the moneys of the integrating areas. It has been suggested, that is to say, that rates of exchange should not merely be adjustable from time to time (as they are to-day under the statutes of the International Monetary Fund) but that they should be allowed to fluctuate day by day, subject to the changing pressures of the exchange markets. In this way, it is argued, balances of payments would be kept in equilibrium by means less disturbing in their effects than the adjustments of internal expenditure which would be necessary if rates of exchange were fixed.

The idea is not without its attractions; and I would not argue that resort to the device of floating rates is inadmissible on any occasion — I can easily think of cases where it would be a most useful expedient. But, from my point of view at any rate, there are serious objections if it is put forward as the basis of a permanent system.

In the first place, in order that it may work at all, it would be necessary for the authorities in the different areas to prohibit all contracts within their area in currencies other than their own. For, if they do not do this, then contracts will tend to be made in terms of the currency which is expected to be most stable, and there will be a tendency for other currencies to depreciate and drop out of use. I think this point deserves more consideration than it has received hitherto. It is a mistake to say that the floating rate is the 'liberal' solution of the problem of inter-local monetary equilibrium. Under pure 'liberalism' there is an obvious tendency for the use of a single medium of exchange to establish itself throughout the whole area of free dealing. There is plenty of confirmation of this, both in present practice and in past currency history. We all know that much more of the business of the world would be done to-day on a dollar basis if it were not for local regulations forbidding such transactions, and there are plenty of historical examples of transactions in a depreciating currency giving way to transactions in a currency expected to be more stable.

Secondly, in my judgment, the device of floating rates involves grave danger of actually *creating* local monetary instability. For it is just not true that, in advanced credit systems, a fluctuation of the rate of exchange brings about equilibrium, if at the same time nothing is done to bring about appropriate tightening or expansion of the internal system. Thus, if the internal credit system is elastic, a fall in the rate of exchange is liable to set up inflationary pressure, unless some brake is applied to internal expansion. Hence, unless the local authorities are alive to this necessity all the time, letting rates float rather than keeping them fixed is liable itself to increase the possibility of instability.

Such considerations surely diminish considerably the charms of the idea of the floating rate as a solution of the problem of inter-local equilibrium. For part of its attractiveness at least arises from the belief that it involves an automatic tendency to equilibration. If it is realized that this is not so, these attractions disappear.

Finally, looking at things from a broader point of view, I must ask, is it not a somewhat odd idea of economic integration which, while bringing about unification of the conditions regulating trade and migration, deliberately leaves the units of account and the media of exchange to national separatism? Is it really to be believed that conditions would be changed for the better, if, in areas already integrated, different monetary systems were allowed to develop in different centres? Would it be an improvement if there existed different monetary systems in each of the forty-eight states of the American union or in each of the constituent parts of the United Kingdom? Would it really make for smoother adjustment to change, less economic instability and a general unification of economic life other than financial payments? I doubt it.

But let no one think that the idea of a common money is itself without difficulties. For, plainly, it involves the most considerable sacrifice of political power on the part of the integrating governments. If there is a common money and a common central bank, the member governments have in effect to give up their power to compel the local banks to create money especially on their behalf. They are in the position of local government or provincial authorities within existing sovereign states. If they want money they must now get it by the same means as are open to other borrowers. They cannot go to the governor of the common central bank and say, 'You *must* create a credit in my favour, otherwise I shall ask for your resignation'. Quite obviously, while there persists a danger of its being involved in war independently of the other members of the association, no existing sovereign state would make such a sacrifice. And, even if there were common arrangements for defence, the surrender of power to coerce local credit arrangements to conform to the requirements of local 'needs' would be a considerable limitation on initiative in general economic policy, and is therefore only likely to be accepted with some reluctance.

Hence I am led to ask, is complete surrender of monetary autonomy the minimum requirement of economic integration? Again perhaps the answer is that it is not absolutely necessary to go quite so far. Looser arrangements, such as the International Monetary Fund statutes or the rules of the European Payments Union, may be regarded as coming under the same heading. That is to say, we can imagine integration taking the form of undertakings to attempt to maintain fixed rates without exchange control and only to alter the rates by common agreement.

Nevertheless, candour compels the admission that such compromises are not easy to work. Experience shows, for instance, that changing rates by agreement is a very difficult undertaking; and there are many signs which suggest a growing recognition of the desirability of more integration rather than less. The recent speech of the Chairman of Lloyds Bank on the possibility of turning the Monetary Fund into a genuine central bank is an important indication of the way the wind is blowing.[1] I think most people who have had most to do with the post-war international monetary institutions would agree that the halfway house is something which must be conceived as being essentially temporary. In the end you must go forward or go back.

VI

Finally, we may ask, what about public finance in relation to integration? To what extent does integration demand the unification of expenditure and taxation?

We may begin with expenditure, and since, at this stage, we are dealing only with economic integration and not political federation, I will leave out all discussion of common military services and ask whether economic integration by itself demands some measure of common expenditure. To which question, in my judgment, the answer is yes, if, in modern conditions, the integration is to have much chance of permanence. But notice that I say 'some measure'. I would not contend, for instance, that complete unification of the so-called social expenditure was something which was at once desirable — although experience within sovereign states points to a tendency in that direction. But I do believe that, if the stresses and strains of adjustment to the new conditions are not to frustrate the intention of integration, some apparatus of compensation funds is desirable. And I would argue, too, that, even when integration has taken

_____
[1] *The Economist*, January 25th, 1958, pp. 350–3.

place, if unity is to be preserved, there must be some scope for this sort of thing. It is indeed one of the main unifying elements within the modern state to-day. We do not allow the incidence of the harsher types of change in different areas to go unmitigated by inter-local transfers, and I believe that, if integration between states is to take place, something similar is probably necessary.

But if this is so, then some source of finance in the shape of common taxation is desirable. If the integration takes the form of the creation of a common customs area, then the proceeds of duties may be available — although some, of course, will be needed to replace what has been surrendered by the integrating states. If it takes the form only of a free-trade area of the kind recently proposed for Western Europe, then other kinds of common levies must be devised; and, in the absence of a central tax-collecting system, this means reliance on local budgets, where it is obvious that co-ordination may be very difficult.

But beyond this, if integration on the lines already discussed is fairly extensive, then a further problem arises on the revenue side — the problem of tax evasion. For it should be clear that the existence of great differences in certain kinds of direct taxes in different parts of the area of integration must be extremely difficult to maintain. You can have differences in the so-called 'beneficial' taxes, that is to say, taxes, the proceeds of which are devoted to improving the value of the real property of the area. But differences in 'onerous' taxes, that is to say, taxes, the expenditure of which has no immediate counterpart in the improvement of real property values — differences in income-tax, for instance — if great, will come more and more to be evaded. For with the destruction of internal customs barriers, the removal of barriers to migration, and the elimination of exchange control, the tendency to evasion of the heavier taxes by living elsewhere must become very strong indeed. Hence, sooner or later, integration must lead to a greater equality in rates of taxation of this sort, and also, I suspect, to some co-ordination of local systems of assessment.

## VII

I now come to my concluding question. So far, at each point in my discussion of different forms of integration, I have enquired concerning the minimum conditions for the realization thereof. And at each stage the answer has run in terms of agreement on common measures : agreement regarding the regulation of trade and migration, agreement regarding the adjustment of rates of exchange, agreement regarding the institution of compensation funds and the raising of the necessary finance. That is to say, I have not argued for the absolute necessity of a clear-cut surrender by the states concerned of all power as regards these functions. I have argued simply that nothing should be done in these spheres by any one of the constituent states save by mutual agreement with the others.

But now, looking cumulatively at these statements of minimum conditions, I am led to ask how probable is long-lasting integration on such terms ? It is easy enough to imagine isolated attempts at integration by *ad hoc* agreement. But is it so easy to imagine that such arrangements will persist year in year out on this basis ?

I will confess freely that I am not very sanguine. Neither in history nor in reason do I see much ground for optimism in this respect.

Let me begin with the evidence of history.

Take first the widest conception of integration. The mid-nineteenth-century free traders clearly thought that once the strength of the argument for freedom of trade was generally realized, world economic integration in the sense of an abolition of barriers to trade and movement would come spontaneously. But, as we know, this did not happen. The argument of the free traders neglected important factors in the situation.[1] They underestimated the influence of the

---

[1] I have dealt with this problem further in the paper on *Liberalism and the International Problem* (below pp. 134-55) and at length in chapter vii of my *Economist in the Twentieth Century*. The short statement here should not be taken to mean to involve endorsement of the arguments commonly used against the nineteenth-century free traders.

infant-industry argument. They underestimated the strength of the pressure groups. They failed to see the real short-run disadvantages which might be involved by unilateral reduction of trade barriers. After a brief interval in which it seemed as if there were some hope for the success of their ideas, the world relapsed into restriction and national separatism.

Or take the more limited idea of integration within the British Commonwealth. From time to time the idea of empire free trade or an imperial *Zollverein* has been mooted. It was suggested by the classical economist Robert Torrens. In our own day, long after there was the remotest chance of it happening, it has been the subject of most energetic propaganda on the part of Lord Beaverbrook and his various organs of publicity. But there has never been much response in other parts of the Commonwealth; and it is pretty safe to say that there never will be. For a brief period, more was done on the limited conception of imperial preference. The famous Ottawa system had its moment of triumph. But it was a growing system only for a very short time, and in recent years it has tended to decline.

Again, take the history of the proposed International Trade Organization, the ambitions of whose founders may perhaps be classified as tending towards a certain kind of economic integration. In its preliminary stages — the diplomatic conversations arising from the famous Article VII of the Lend-Lease Agreement between the United States and the United Kingdom — it seemed as though there was a reasonable hope of something being achieved on these lines. But when international conferences got down to the details of drafting the charter, the simplicity of the original idea was completely snowed under by the complications of the let-out clauses insisted upon by different members and different pressure groups ; and in the end the thing was bogged down and abandoned. Happily, the more limited outcome of the preliminary negotiations, the excellent G.A.T.T. organization, survives, and its small and devoted secretariat do splendid work. But it is always under challenge. There is no guarantee of persistence in such arrangements.

I will not say that all experience tends in this direction. But the only really conspicuous example of successful economic integration without political union was the German *Zollverein*; and when this is closely examined it proves to be the kind of exception which, on analysis, vindicates the rule. For few things can be more certain in history than that, if the *Zollverein* had not been backed at each stage by the predominant political influence of Prussia, it would never have survived the various crises which accompanied its existence. I do not think that it is possible for believers in economic integration without political union to draw much consolation from this case.

If we consider the broad politics of the situation, the reason for all this disappointing experience is not very far to seek : our minimum conditions of integration involve continuing agreement between independent sovereign states.

Now it is easy enough to conceive agreements made at one point of time, and we know that such agreements frequently take place. But the continued existence of co-operative arrangements, when, if the thing is to hang together, agreement on each issue arising is more or less essential, is not so easy to conceive ; and the permanence of such arrangements does not seem to me to be much more probable than the stability of any political system which requires unanimity. In the international sphere, it seems to me, the likelihood of continuing harmony, in arrangements between completely independent sovereign states, is not much greater than was the likelihood of continuity of internal government under the rule of *liberum veto*.

Hence I am forced to the conclusion that integration on a thoroughgoing scale is not likely to have permanent viability without much more surrender of political sovereignty than is implied by my minimum conditions. The pure logic of *The Federalist* has never been refuted, and I think it is supported by the verdict of history. Neither in the economic nor in the military sphere are we likely to succeed in adapting the political structure of the West to the requirements of modern conditions without much more far-reaching political reconstruction than at present many of us are willing to contemplate.

But does all this imply hostility to more limited efforts? Does my deep-seated conviction that in the end we must get something like a full-blooded federation mean that I wish to blow cold on more limited experiments in this direction? Not at all. We live through time; and if, for a time, systems which ultimately break down, succeed in effecting temporary improvement, that is so much gained. I do not underrate at all the value of some of the experimentation in this sphere in recent years. It may have fostered some delusions. It may have distracted attention from some fundamental issues. But it has prevented some evils; and it has created a great fund of experience and knowledge which is good in itself and which could be of great use if we were willing to go forward. All that I contend is that, sooner or later, somehow or other, if the Western World is to achieve a greater integration, its present organization into independent sovereign states must give way to something larger. I am sure this is true where military security is concerned, and it has been the argument of this lecture that it is equally true of integration in the economic sphere.

# 7

## LIBERALISM AND THE
## INTERNATIONAL PROBLEM [1]

### I

THIS paper is in the nature of an inquest — an inquest on the inadequacy of an idea. Most men of my age, at any rate in the English-speaking world, were brought up against a background of nineteenth-century liberalism. Whatever party we supported in general elections, the general system of thought deriving from this period informed our ideas. Much of the political speculation of our own age has been a revision or reformulation of its aims. It has therefore occurred to me that it would be a suitable subject for this lecture, to enquire a little what was the liberal outlook in relation to the problem of international relations and to what extent it has proved adequate. This is not a theme which I would regard as appropriate to all audiences outside my own country. But in the land of Mazzini and Croce, I trust that I may be understood.

### II

Let me begin with the historic function and achievement of this movement.

The essence of the liberalism of the enlightenment was the freeing of the individual. We need not enquire too closely into the diverse historical influences — the evolution of law as a by-product of constitutional struggle, as in England ; the doctrine of natural rights and the ardours of revolutionary change as in France. The important thing is that everywhere the practical manifestation of these influences was

---

[1] This is the substance of an address delivered before the *Società Italiana per la Organizzazione Internazionale* at Rome in the spring of 1960.

the destruction of limitations on individual initiative — the
emancipation of serfs, the consolidation of the rule of law,
the removal of restrictions on trade and movement, the
establishment of liberty of speech and publication. And let
no one think of this as a negative achievement. The institutions of a free society had become so much part and parcel of
the ordinary texture of life in the west, that until in our own
day they have come under threat from Fascist and Communist tyranny, we have been apt to take them for granted.
But if anyone should doubt what liberalism meant in
positive spiritual terms, let him read Shelley's *Prometheus
Unbound* or, better still, listen to the chorus of the prisoners in
*Fidelio*.

But now it is important to note that all this involved a
strong state. It is quite fundamental to any proper understanding of historical liberalism to realize that it was not
anarchistic. Philosophical anarchism has indeed played a
not inconsiderable rôle in the history of European thought :
whatever we may think of its ultimate validity it would be
wrong to underestimate the influence of men such as Godwin
and Kropotkin. But, although it is sometimes confused with
liberalism, in fact it is to be sharply distinguished. Liberalism may well have urged the abolition of state intervention
in many walks of life. It may have ridiculed the claims of
states to create happiness or of collective entities to transcend
the experience of the individuals of which they were composed. But even in its most *laissez-faire* form — and much
liberalism, including that of the English classical economists,
was not *laissez-faire* in the popular sense of the term — it
demanded a strong state. The rule of law, so conspicuous a
feature of the liberal conception, could not be maintained
without an effective apparatus of coercion. The famous
harmony of individual actions was only a harmony because
legal restraints and institutions created an arena in which
it might emerge. Moreover — a circumstance not always
noticed — the liberal reforms often involved the state taking
over functions up to then discharged by private enterprise.
The liberal conception of an orderly society had no room for

private police or armies, the farming out of tax collection, colonizing companies with unlimited rights, and so on.

This being so, it is something of a paradox that, when dealing with international problems, liberalism should have adopted a different attitude. Where relations between different states were concerned, there indeed its attitude became that of philosophical anarchism. The assumption seems to have been, that if the different states were all to adopt internal liberal policies, then a general harmony of interests would be established in which wars and friction would cease and perpetual peace be established. It is not so easy to find a systematic statement of this view among liberal thinkers; and of course there were important exceptions who showed deeper insight. But it would be difficult to deny that something of this sort was the inspiration of important political parties. John Bright and Cobden would certainly have subscribed to something of this sort. Indeed, before 1914, it was the implicit view of perhaps a majority of English liberals — it was a disaster for the world that it was so.

Now we know — to our cost — that this view was a delusion. It was a delusion for exactly the same reason that philosophical anarchism is a delusion: it leaves out of account the possibility of anti-social action. If there were no statesmen and soldiers with different conceptions of the world; if *all* states restricted their activities to the liberal prescriptions; if there were no obstacles to trade and the movement of capital and labour and no attempt to create positions of special privilege, then doubtless the state of affairs contemplated would prevail: one international society, practising division of labour, with the different states performing, as it were, the functions of unco-ordinated but harmonious local government authorities; and there would be no need for any international authority — just as, if all individuals within the nation spontaneously restricted their activities to socially compatible aims, there would be no need for internal law or police. But, unfortunately, we know that all states do not conceive their functions thus, any more than all individuals, and that if some do not, then the mere force of self-interest may compel others to adopt a different attitude. And this delusion had the tragic effect that for many years — years in which it might have been easier to do better — little or no attempt was made to provide a superior system. Throughout the liberal period, the international anarchy prevailed, and in the end it went up in smoke and destroyed much of liberalism with it.

Why was this? Why did so many of the best and purest minds of the nineteenth century conceive the international problem in such simplisitic terms?

The answer is complex. Partly, no doubt, it was pure ignorance springing from a certain type of temperament. I think it is true to say that many liberals of this period had a singularly naïve view of human nature. In the calm epoch of the nineteenth century they tended to think that international ill-will, ambition, and doctrinaire crusading were things of the past; the world was so enlightened that major wars were not at all probable. Certainly this was the belief of the sweet and wholesome society in which I grew up as a boy. How well I remember the dismay, the horrified amazement of my elders in August 1914, when, out of the summer blue, they suddenly realized that this was not so. It is one of the important facts of history that so widespread was this belief among liberals in the United Kingdom, that the Liberal Ministers of the day, who knew better the perilous equilibrium of the world, feared to tell their followers and so were prevented from making the declarations which might have prevented the catastrophe.

But it was not all temperament and ignorance: there were intellectual and spiritual influences tending the same way. Two of these in particular deserve our attention: first an oversimplified view of economic possibilities in the international sphere; secondly, the historic alliance of liberalism with nationalism and the idea of self-determination. It is the main purpose of this paper to elucidate this a little. The two central sections therefore will deal with these influences. Then, by way of conclusion, I shall ask shortly where

137

liberalism should stand to-day in regard to the international problem.

III

I turn first to oversimplification of economic possibilities. And let me say at once that what I am undertaking must not be thought to be a history or a critique of technical thought on these matters. It is clear that most of the points over-looked by the attitude I am discussing were explicitly recog-nized by one or other of the classical economists, even if their implications for policy were not always underlined or perhaps completely realized.[1] The trouble was that the popularizers overlooked these points and were thus led to an over-simple view of the political problem.

Let us begin with finance. The liberal reaction against earlier economic policies — the policies which sometimes go by the somewhat ambiguous name of mercantilism — began by the denunciation of measures designed to turn the balance of payments in favour of the nation concerned. It had been feared that in the absence of such measures a country would be drained of its gold and silver; and it was one of the most conspicuous achievements of David Hume that, on the assumption of common metallic standards and no banking to speak of, he showed the baselessness of fears in this re-spect. In such circumstances — virtually those of a common currency — he showed that something like a self-righting mechanism operated: if there were a continuous loss of metal, there would be a fall of prices and incomes and a consequential increase of exports and diminution of imports; if there were a continuous inflow, symmetrically contrary movement would take place. All economists must remember his comparison of trade between countries and trade between counties or provinces, and the immortal passage in which he surmised that 'had the Heptarchy subsisted in *England*, the legislature of each state had been continually alarmed by the fear of a wrong balance, and as it is probable that the

---

[1] For a fuller treatment of this part of the subject I may perhaps refer to my *Economist in the Twentieth Century*, especially chapters v-viii.

mutual hatred of these states would have been extremely violent on account of their close neighbourhood, they would have loaded and oppressed all commerce by a jealous and superfluous caution'.[1]

This demonstration made a deep impression — as well it might — and became one of the intellectual spearheads of the attack on restrictive systems. Indeed, so deeply embodied did it become in the liberal *Weltanschaung* that, even in my own lifetime, I have heard a prominent liberal economist argue as if all talk of a balance-of-payment problem was pure moonshine.[2]

But of course this was not at all true. Hume's demonstration was all right on his assumptions — a common metallic currency and no banks. But introduce the serpent of bank credit into this Eden, allow independent centres of money manufacture as we have in modern states and the situation is very different. In such circumstances, only if the manufacture of money obeys certain rules of expansion and contraction proportionate to the inflow and outflow of metal can one assume the existence of a self-righting mechanism. And, of course, given independent central bank and independent governments with independent financial policies, there is no guarantee at all that these rules will be observed.

All this is also in Hume. With the uncanny insight of a truly great genius, he perceived that the development of banking, then in its infancy, could upset his harmony. 'I scarcely know any method', he said, 'of sinking money below its level but those institutions of banks and funds and paper credit which are so much practised in this kingdom. These render paper equivalent to money . . . make it supply the place of gold and silver, raise proportionately the price of labour and commodities, by that means either lose a great part of these precious metals or prevent their further increase.'[3] But the popularizers did not notice this and the doctrine of the self-righting mechanism became the accepted

---

[1] *Essays, Moral, Political and Literary*, Ed. Green and Grose, vol. i, p. 337.
[2] See the quotation from Edwin Cannan in my Stamp Lecture on *The Balance of Payments* (Athlone Press), p. 6.       [3] *Op. cit.* p. 335.

liberal interpretation of the world, so that when, in 1930, Keynes called it in question they just did not know what to say. What they should have said was *not* that a self-righting mechanism always existed, but rather that, if one were to be constructed, it should base itself upon Hume's model — that is a state of affairs in which payments between different currency areas conformed to the pattern which would exist if there were one currency area only. That *au fond* was what the intellectual architects of the Bank Act of 1844 were really trying to do, inadequate as were their conceptions of means and mechanisms. But, for the most part, insights of this sort found no part in the broad teaching of liberalism on international economic relations.

During the greater part of the nineteenth century and up to 1914, probably this did not matter very much. Under metallic standards the extent to which the rules were departed from in the major centres was not often very important. Minor areas got into trouble. South American countries provide classic examples of balance-of-payments difficulties due to inappropriate monetary policies, but the extent to which the rest of the world was upset was small. Moreover, so much of the trade of the world was financed on sterling bills, that London tended to set the pace all round, and *de facto* there was much more of an international currency managed from one centre than there ever existed *de jure*.

But, with the break-up of this system in 1914, these somewhat freak conditions came to an end. The different monetary centres pursued different policies and any pre-established harmony or self-righting mechanism was conspicuous by its absence. No one was justified in saying in those years that there were no balance-of-payments problems. In recent years there has been some slight improvement. But in so far as this has happened, it has been, in part at least, the result of the deliberate creation of special international arrangements involving some surrender of national initiative — the European Clearing Union, the International Monetary Fund, the Bankers' Club at Basle. All these can well be thought to be in harmony with the spirit of liberalism. But they involve a very considerable modification of the thought of the so-called liberal period.

Let us turn now to matters of trade. Here the intellectual background of the traditional liberal attitude is perhaps even more considerable than that which we have just been examining. Adam Smith's famous demonstration of the benefits flowing from industrial division of labour was soon recognized to apply also to division of labour between areas. And the conception of the benefits here involved, by what Robert Torrens called the territorial division of labour, was given an even sharper edge by the development of the theory of comparative cost — an insight so comprehensive, so profound, that an economist of our own day, Ludwig von Mises, has been led to describe it as the law of social union itself (*Vergesellschaftungsgesetz*).[1] When this was further conjoined with the Ricardian theory of the distribution of the precious metals, the working of a system of economic freedom in the international sphere seemed to stand out bold and clear. Certainly, whatever its elisions and concealed assumptions, it was one of the most impressive achievements in the whole history of social thought. Small wonder that the liberals of the day were apt to think the intellectual argument to be all on their side.

Nevertheless, in assuming that the authorities of the different national states would refrain from action which would impede the realization of this harmony, the liberals of that day overlooked a number of important elements in the situation.

They overlooked, first, the strength of producer interest. The classical analysis suggested a benefit to all from free trade save for the owners of specialized instruments and specialized skills. But this assumed mobility of capital and labour and the will to such mobility. If this assumption was not justified, then clearly changes in the conditions of international supply and demand might involve damage to the position of particular groups, and, in any case, impediments

[1] *Nationalökonomie* (Geneva, 1940), pp. 126 *seq.*

to trade might imply benefits. The interest of organized producers therefore frequently might point to restriction : and if this was so, there was not reason to suppose that they would refrain from pressing this interest.

Considerations of this sort are pretty obvious. But traditional liberalism held that, since such groups were a minority, there was no reason to believe that they would eventually get their way. Once the benefits of freedom were generally realized, producer interest would dash its head in vain against the resistance of the consumers. The history of the repeal of the Corn Laws was held to provide justification for this attitude.

We know now that this was a pathetic fallacy. The interest of producers is almost always more active than that of consumers, and their encroachments have to be pretty blatant before much attempt is made to resist them. It is no use pointing to the crude fallacy and flagrant intellectual dishonesty of most of the special pleading : the experience of democracy all over the world is that standards are not severe in this respect. Moreover, it is important to recognize that there are often times when the interests of special groups in regard to trade restriction can quite plausibly be made to appear to coincide with the interests of the community at large. If unemployment is at all extensive, then measures which appear to create employment anywhere or to prevent more unemployment, very easily commend themselves to harassed politicians and the electorate, even though the long run effects are bad and likely to persist long after the unemployment has passed away. British industry is still among the most highly protected among the advanced nations of the world, although the unemployment of the thirties which gave rise to our high protectionism has long disappeared and the unemployment percentage has seldom been much more than two, and very often considerably less.

But beyond this there was a further oversight which from the speculative, if not the practical, point of view was even more disturbing. It was not clearly recognized, indeed it was often not recognized at all, that situations were conceivable when the imposition of restriction might benefit the national group and repeal of restriction be damaging. I am not here referring to the possibility that infant industries may be fostered by protection: the analytical basis of this famous argument had been elaborated and made respectable by no less an authority than John Stuart Mill, although he had repented of the use made by it by private interest and had argued that what protection was involved was better provided by subsidies than by tariffs. I am referring rather to the possibility that geographical groups acting, as it were, monopolistically might be able to turn the terms of trade in their favour and thus secure a greater share of the benefits from trade.

This possibility had been recognized comparatively early by the classical economists. But with the exception of Robert Torrens, who regarded it as an argument against unilateral free trade and in favour of an imperial *Zollverein*,[1] the tendency was to dismiss it as unimportant. Alfred Marshall, who certainly was very careful not to compromise himself with the more specious popular arguments for freedom of trade, argued strongly that, *in the long run*, for the majority of advanced societies, the elasticities of demand and supply of the goods they dealt in, were not likely to promise much from this kind of restriction and that the dangers of actual loss were quite considerable.

No doubt there is much in this attitude; I have never seen a refutation of Marshall's argument in this connection. But unfortunately, as a possible influence on day-to-day policy, it cannot be regarded as very cogent. For, whereas in the long run, it may well be true that gains of this sort are very unlikely, it is not so easy to make this assertion of the short run, where the elasticities of demand and supply may well be less and the possibilities of gain or loss very much greater. And this applies particularly to the repeal of restrictions. The politician would be courageous indeed who would risk a short-run loss by the unilateral lowering

---

[1] See my *Robert Torrens and the Evolution of Classical Political Economy*, chapter vii, *passim*.

of tariffs, even though in the long run there was no danger
of this sort and a prospect of substantial gain.

Anyway, here is an argument which blurs the axiomatic
simplicity of the pure liberal case for unilateral free trade.
And if we take this into account and all the special pleading
which can be mustered in support of special interest, it is
not difficult to see that, where power to restrict exists, there
it is often likely to be employed, and that a condition in
which, without deliberate supra-national contrivance, there
prevails a general absence of restriction, is not likely before
the Greek Kalends. It was a beautiful vision, but not of this
world.

I find it odd that all this was not more generally realized
by the nineteenth-century liberals. After all, it was one of
their great achievements to have swept away the internal
obstacles to trade, the *octrois*, the tolls, the laws of settlement,
and so on. They did not leave this to the operation of self-
interest on the part of the different *local* authorities, the
municipalities, the feudal lords, the parishes. They would
have ridiculed the idea that, if power to restrict were left
in the hands of such authorities it would never be used
— whether as a result of the pressure of sinister interest or
transitory emergency. They would have been foremost in
resisting attempts to restore such powers, and they would
have spurned any attempt, in the alleged interest of the
sacred cause of local self-government, to defeat their concentration in the hands of the central state.

Why then were they so little interested in combating
such powers in the hands of *national* authorities? Why this
facile optimistic reliance on reason and persuasion unassisted
by appropriate institutions? Why this tendency to regard
the nation as something ultimate?

Partly no doubt because of the great practical difficulties
of creating anything superior. Doubtless, if our question
had been put to a really intelligent liberal, such as J. S. Mill,
the reply would have been that the nation was but a temporary expedient pending the creation of a wider spirit of
world solidarity. Our intelligent liberal would not have

argued that there was any special virtue in the international anarchy. But he would have argued that there was little that could be done about it.

But while this would have been reasonable enough in itself, it is doubtful whether it can be regarded as the whole truth. For what needs explanation here is not merely why no more was achieved, but further, why no more was attempted; and beyond this, and even more significant, why there were no more warnings of the implications of contemporary tendencies. Why, where the British Empire was concerned, did liberals stand by without protest as it disintegrated into more or less totally independent units? Why were not more apprehensions expressed concerning the separatist tendencies within other states elsewhere?

Doubtless, there are many reasons: no single explanation is adequate. But I am convinced that one very important reason is to be found in the alliance, during that period, of liberalism and nationalism and the almost hypnotic influence exercised on the liberal mind by the word self-government.

But this brings me to the next division of my subject.

IV

It is not at all difficult to understand the initial reasons for this alliance. The early nationalist struggles were struggles against domination and discrimination: the members of the rebellious groups, although obviously of equal intelligence and culture with the members of the ruling powers, were limited in their rights as regards law-making and administration — or they had no rights at all. This was obviously a state of restricted personal liberty and as such clearly quite incompatible with the liberal idea. It was the most natural thing in the world for English liberals such as Byron and Shelley to sympathize with the struggles for freedom in Italy and Greece.

But it is one thing to demand equal citizenship and the abolition of discrimination: it is quite another to claim separation from the political union and the creation of new sovereign bodies. No doubt, in the two instances I have mentioned, there were very good reasons why separation was the only practical solution — though I am pretty clear that this was not necessarily so with other separatist movements. But separatism is not in itself a liberal solution. It is logically quite distinct and, from the liberal point of view, can at best be regarded as a *pis aller*. Moreover, and this is the point to which I have been directing my exposition, it is easily capable of being the vehicle of an entirely different ideology.

For plainly, if the plea for separation is not merely a plea for a practical absence of discrimination and common rights under the law, but rather a plea for the expression of specific differences, we enter a new world of conceptions and one in which objectives which are the reverse of liberal can very easily flourish. It is the essence of liberalism, by providing legal systems equally applicable to all, to ensure scope for individual difference and variety, an objective which is the exact contrary to that which seizes on accidental dissimilarities of race or language as a pretext for the multiplication of different legal codes. And this is no mere academic distinction. On a very practical plane, in areas of mixed population, separatist claims for the expression of differences have often led simply to a shift in the incidence of discrimination and ascendancy; and, on the ideological plane, they can speedily lead to the apotheosis of the collective entity as such, the chosen race, the bearers of destiny — with all the horrific and contemptible consequences which in our time we know only too well. A liberal may well decide that in the interests of peace and the continuity of the going concern, he must acquiesce in the persistence of existing differences in the legal and political structure of the affairs of humanity. But to regard them as something good in themselves, rather than a perpetual occasion of danger, is to be blind to the lesson of history and indifferent to liberal values. It is not for liberals to regard the Curse of Babel as a blessing.

Moreover, even in its more moderate manifestations, the

separatist idea very easily becomes tainted with another which is equally alien to the most fundamental conceptions of liberalism — the idea of national sovereignty and its inviolability. And hence comes the dogma of the fundamental equality of states — which in our own time has led to the crowning absurdity of voting arrangements at international assemblies which give equal votes to, say, Panama and the United States of America. Indeed, such is the muddlement of minds on this matter, that I have even heard criticism of the principle of one state one vote described as anti-liberal and anti-democratic — as though arrangements which give the citizen of the larger states a smaller proportionate influence than the citizen of the smaller states were themselves anything but the total reverse of liberalism and democracy.[1]

But there is an even more insidious way in which the idea of the right of self-determination comes into conflict with the fundamental liberal postulates. For, in the last analysis, it is an attack on the principle of the necessary minimum of authority which we saw to be an essential ingredient in the liberal conception of an ordered society. If just any collection of people have the right to get together and dissociate themselves from wider authority, not because they are not accorded equal rights, but merely because they want to assert their differences, then there is no longer any cohesive principle in the world. You are faced with a vicious circle. The inhabitants of a certain area claim the right of secession and of complete self-government. They are supported by droves of unreflecting liberals. Independence is achieved, but the inhabitants of a certain department within the new state regard themselves as prejudiced

---

[1] It is this sort of arrangement which makes the United Nations so much less serious and effective an organization than the International Monetary Fund or the International Bank, whose voting systems do at least make some attempt to take account of contemporary realities. But the point I am trying to make here concerns not the practical suitability of different voting systems but rather their moral standing. And what the apologists of U.N. will not see is that there is no moral basis in liberalism or democracy for their present arrangement, and that, with the almost indefinite proliferation of small states in the present age, the thing becomes more and more absurd.

by the new arrangements. Accordingly, they, too, claim the right to contract out. New liberal support is attracted. Intolerable wrongs and injustices are paraded, and, after more commotion, a further state is carved out. And so on *ad infinitum*. It is the world of philosophical anarchism, not liberalism. There is nowhere to draw the line.

Doubtless, things are not always as bad as this. Much that has fed the ardours of separatist movements has been purely subjective or sinister — the second-rate enthusiasms of philologists, personal ambition on the part of dynamic men, or the pressure of economic interests. But no one would deny some broad differences of historical evolution justifying some separation, and some ancient grievances which make unified living together exceptionally difficult : no one in his senses would urge that the Anglo-Indian problem could possibly have been settled by giving every Indian the right to elect a representative at Westminster ! But objective elements of this sort can be over emphasized. The degree to which my picture of the vicious circle is a burlesque is easily capable of exaggeration. There is much more of the purely irrational and chaotic in the break-up of the world than the representatives of contemporary national groups would agree — especially as regards Europe and the Atlantic Community.

In any case — and this is the point I wish to stress — the clash of principle is a real one. It is not a figment of the theoretical fancy. It has involved tragic conflicts in history. Think, for instance, of the war between the states in North America. To me it is always one of the outstanding paradoxes of the history of thought that, of all statesmen of the last hundred and fifty years, the figure which would probably command the most instant emotional devotion and admiration from liberals of all lands — at any rate on this side of the Atlantic — would be Abraham Lincoln — perhaps the one great figure of nineteenth-century political history who survives the acid of historical criticism. Men who would foam at the mouth at my denigration of Wilsonian principle would be united on this. Yet it was Lincoln who was prepared to unloose the most terrible civil war in nineteenth-century history *not*, be it remembered, to emancipate the slaves — that was a by-product of strategy which, in the absence of war, might have been deferred a long time — but rather to preserve the Union from disintegration.

V

All that I have been saying so far relates to types of thought which, even if they continue to influence events, tend to-day to appear outmoded : the main purpose of the exercise has been to examine the reasons for an ideological misfire. Perhaps, before coming to an end, it is not out of place to add one or two morals for contemporary practice. If we still believe in the general idea of a liberal society, what should be our attitude at the present day to the grand problem of relations between nations ? Needless to say, we must still continue on a plane of great generality : even less than before, there can be no question of comment on particular issues of day-to-day policy.

The first point which I should like to emphasize is the necessity of recognition that, here as elsewhere, if there is to be liberty there must also be order. This is just as true of the relations between individuals and groups of individuals living in different states as it is of similar relations within states. And if there is to be order, then there must also be authority. It is pure delusion to suppose that in a free society *everything* can be arranged by specific and voluntary agreements. Doubtless in present international conditions we often have to rely on mere agreements — voluntary alliances or associations from which withdrawal is possible — and it would be folly to ignore what can be done in this way or to refrain from attempting to do it because something better is conceivable. But when all is said and done, this kind of thing is essentially a *pis aller* ; and in modern conditions it is just not good enough. To create lasting harmony authority is essential.

But what kind of authority ? It is perhaps hardly

149

necessary to say that in our day at least the idea of a unitary world state is utterly impracticable. It is inconceivable that it should come about spontaneously; only conquest on a scale never yet known in history could establish it, and even then it is pretty certain that eventually it would break down. But even if this were not so, even if a world state of this kind were practicable, in my judgment it would be highly undesirable. Only if the functions of the state are conceived to be limited to those of the pure night watchman would it be tolerable to contemplate. As soon as other functions are assumed — and I hasten to say that I think they should be assumed — then the idea that they should all be concentrated in a single hand becomes highly distasteful, to put it mildly — think, for instance, of the complete concentration in the hands of one world ministry of the educational function. As I have said already, I see no virtue in international anarchy. But provided there is some central preservation of law and order, I see much virtue in decentralized initiative. The philosophy of liberalism builds much on the decentralized initiative of individuals and groups which is made possible by the institutions of private and corporate property. There is another chapter to be written on the importance, from this point of view, of the decentralized initiative of local government bodies *including*, in the world of the future, the local government bodies which at present are sovereign states.

It is considerations of this sort which make the idea of federation so attractive.[1] For the main principle here, as I understand things, is *the surrender of sovereignty in certain specified fields*. The federal authority has sole power in regard to defence, regulation of trade between states and with the outside world, and such-like functions; but, once

[1] In this connection I may perhaps be permitted to refer to my own *Economic Planning and International Order*, published in 1936. Although there is much in this book which I would now phrase differently, I still hold to the main principles of the arguments for international federalism there elaborated. I claim no originality in this respect. The derivation from the *Federalist* is unmistakable, although the development of the argument may be different. But I take some retrospective pleasure in its appearance some years before the better-known modern works on this subject.

a certain restricted catalogue of functions is exhausted, initiative and jurisdiction remain with the federating states. For me at least this is the dominating and essential characteristic. The constitution of the federal authority, its mode of election and so on, are matters which are doubtless extremely important. But, so long as this central feature is retained, these can vary a good deal without the essential characteristic being lost. I am inclined, for reasons which I have already developed, to think that federalism thus conceived is a good thing in itself — a truly liberal solution. And I am convinced that in the long run it will prove to be the only permanent solution of the problem of international order.

In saying this I have no wish to decry other expedients. We live from day to day and the all-or-nothing attitude, here, as in most other walks of life, is not only slightly ridiculous but also very sterile. Certainly I would be the last to wish to undervalue the devoted labours of recent years in non-federal international institutions or to deny some utility to the general process of getting mixed-up in enterprises of good-will. I would only argue that these things are dangerous if they tend to foster the belief that they are in themselves enough — if they tend to blur our vision of the ultimate objective. We should not depend on associations of comparable fragility and lack of power in *internal* affairs, and in the end we ought not to be content with them in the world at large. For the liberal outlook at least, whatever compromises or makeshifts we have to put up with on the way, it is a federal solution which must be the ultimate goal.

But, having said this, I should like to say also — and this especially to friends in the official federalist movements — that it is very important that the idea should not degenerate into a parrot formula and a substitute for further thought. We must not suppose that human invention is exhausted and that world federation on the United States model is the only way of realizing our central idea and the only conceivable goal for the immediate future. For federation of that sort and on that scale must depend upon certain pre-conditions not always prevailing either in space or in time, of which perhaps two in particular deserve special emphasis.

First, there must be adequate communication between the areas to be federated. This is no obstacle to-day, when you can travel from London to New York in six hours. But it was enormously important historically. Adam Smith's project of an empire embracing both the American colonies and the United Kingdom was a splendid vision. But, even had there been the will to carry it out, which was notoriously absent on both sides of the Atlantic — it would probably have broken down because of the slowness of sea transport.

But, secondly, and much more important, there must exist a certain minimum degree of likemindedness between the powers surrendering sovereign functions. You cannot begin to create federal power if there exists complete dis-agreement on the objectives and ideals in the service of which federal power may be used. You will not surrender control of your destiny to majorities whose intentions and whose conceptions of the true ends of life you fear to be inimical to your own.

It is this, of course, which in our day and age renders impracticable any idea of world federation with normal federal powers. For, at least from the point of view of those communities which practise the traditions of western liberal civilization, it must be recognized that there are large areas of the surface of this planet inhabited by communities, in the aggregate with superior numbers, whose conceptions of human aims and interests are so very different from ours that this degree of living together is not yet conceivable. It may be that recognition of the immense danger to the human race as a whole of certain military weapons may bring about a willingness to submit their control to a common authority more speedily than at present seems likely — as Dr. Johnson said, if a man is condemned to be hanged, it is extraordinary how much it concentrates his thoughts. But more than this it is impossible to hope for yet awhile. It is possible that, as the years go on, the intense proselytizing zeal of the totalitarian régimes may burn itself out and the intelligent youth, bored with the ancient slogans, may come to see less of an enemy in the ideals of the free society, in which case more comprehensive combinations might be hoped for. But that time is not yet. As things are at present, men would fight not to join such a union rather than to join it.

If, therefore, we are to think in terms of potential like-mindedness and the preservation of liberal values, I am pretty clear that in the immediate future at least the maximum area is the area of what is sometimes called the Atlantic Community, *i.e.* the United States, Western Europe, and certain, but not all, parts of the Commonwealth.[1] And, to my personal way of thinking at least, such a union over such an area would be perfectly acceptable ; it would be a union of peoples with common standards of justice, common economic techniques and a common culture to preserve and advance. Moreover, speaking as a citizen of the United Kingdom, with its peculiar ties with certain extra-European communities, it would be an area in which complete and wholehearted co-operation would be easier than in any other. Anything less would be imperfect in one way or another, anything more, liable to break down through lack of likemindedness.

But is it likely? I doubt if the United States is ready : isolationism is not that much defeated. Since the war the citizens of that much-abused country have displayed a generosity in cash and a personal devotion to abstract causes without precedent in human history, but hitherto they have been lacking in the creative imagination which led to their own union. Moreover, during the same period, in the United Kingdom there have been too many labouring under what, in my judgment, are essentially erroneous ideas concerning the present-day potentialities of the Commonwealth, and again and again we have shown ourselves blind to our

---

[1] The phrasing is intentionally ambiguous. If I were to be challenged as to my basis of selection, the answer would be simple — willingness to surrender sovereignty in matters of foreign policy, defence, and the regulation of inter-state trade, immigration, and finance. I leave it to my readers to decide how much of the Commonwealth is eligible on this criterion.

real interest in larger, and, in the long run, more viable conceptions. Finally, in Western Europe there has developed a period of intense preoccupation with the formation of union on a more limited scale. We of the United Kingdom have missed many opportunities to lay the foundations of what for us would be the more advantageous Atlantic Union : and it may be that, for the time being, the possibility has receded and we shall have to be content with more limited constructions less congenial to the heart's desire.

But it is always difficult to peer into the future, and, just now especially, prediction is a fool's game. In the present chaos of the world, who knows how the kaleidoscope will look next? The one thing of which I feel sure is the thought which has been the leading contention of this lecture, namely, that where law is not enforceable by sanctions, there, there can be no true liberty. We shall not establish complete freedom on earth until we have established a rule of law and an appropriate structure of government.

## NOTE

What is said in the penultimate paragraph above indicates a change of view which perhaps ought to be made more explicit. In the ten years after the war, while strongly supporting the idea of Atlantic Union, I was definitely opposed to the idea that the United Kingdom should join a purely European community — the curious will find my reasons in a paper in my *Economist in the Twentieth Century*. I was in favour of attempting to move towards the larger union by developing the framework and institutions of the North Atlantic Alliance. But much has happened since then ; opportunities have been missed and one fatal mistake has changed irrevocably our standing in the world. I therefore now incline to the view that such developments, although still very desirable and indeed greatly to be preferred to integrations within a more limited area, are too distant to provide the speedy consolidation we need ; and so, although not at all blind to the disadvantages and dangers, I am in favour of our application to join the Common Market and I accept the further political implications which this may have. I should like to take this opportunity of expressing regret for a disparaging reference, in the paper alluded to above, to M. Monnet's initiatives in this connection. The march of events has shown M. Monnet's plans to have been more practical than those put forward by those of us who opposed him; and if eventually there should take place that Union of the West which is so necessary if we are to survive, it should be acknowledged that it will have owed much to his vision and devotion.

# PART III

# 8

# MACDOUGALL ON THE
# DOLLAR PROBLEM [1]

## I

ANY work by Sir Donald MacDougall must command the most respectful attention, both from his fellow economists and from the general public. He was one of Sir Winston Churchill's economic advisers during the war and again between 1951 and 1953; he has been an Economics Director of the Organization for European Economic Co-operation; and, as an academic economist at Oxford, he has made notable contributions to the advancement of his subject. The appearance, therefore, of this most extensive book, coming, as it does, at a time [2] when in many parts of the world there are apprehensions of a re-emergence of dollar shortage, must be regarded as an event of some importance. Whatever our degree of agreement with Sir Donald's conclusions, he surely deserves the gratitude of us all for the truly monumental labours which have gone to his arguments and computations. A solid, even-tempered discussion of one of the most important issues of the day.

## II

The dollar problem, as Sir Donald conceives it, is essentially a balance-of-payments problem. 'Is the rest of the world, over the next decade or two, likely to have chronic or recurring difficulties in balancing its accounts with the U.S.?' (p. 23). That is how he poses the question.

---

[1] A review article, originally printed in *Crossbow*, January 1958, on 'The World Dollar Problem. A Study in International Economics' by Sir Donald MacDougall. Apart from a purely formal change in the structure of one sentence, the text is printed as originally published.    [2] 1955.

And he defines a solution 'as a situation in which the rest of the world has an easy balance of payments with the U.S. on current account, but allowing for all grants and capital movements other than U.S. Government aid which has as an important objective the relief of dollar shortage' (p. 27).

Accepting this formulation, it is clear that the simplest way for general dollar shortage to arise would be by way of deflation in the U.S. If, the rest of the world being on a more or less even keel, neither inflating nor deflating the volume of expenditure in the U.S. were to slacken notice-ably, then obviously there would tend to be a slackening in the supply of dollars coming forward, and, in the absence of adequate reserves in the centres concerned, there would be real difficulty in settling U.S. accounts. Sir Donald deals with all this in a very satisfactory way. I agree with his view that, although American depressions of pre-war severity are not very likely, it would be folly to expect that from time to time depressions of a minor order will not occur. I agree with him too in his emphasis upon the extreme insufficiency to deal with such influences of the present reserve position in most of the rest of the world, particularly the sterling area.

Exactly similar reasoning goes to show how dollar shor-tage must result if, other things being equal, the rest of the world *in*flates. Sir Donald's analysis makes this equally clear. But the plan he has adopted for the greater part of his argument, of lumping together the various countries of the rest of the world and only dealing at length with 'regional' differences near the end when the main divisions of analysis have become a little blurred with the complexity of refine-ments, inhibits him from driving home the applications as vividly as might be wished. An enquiry why some countries have *not* had a dollar problem in recent years would reveal, I suspect, in some cases though not all, that it has been to some extent because they have not inflated as much as others. And, speaking generally, I cannot resist the feeling that in any practical analysis of post-war history this factor deserves a good deal more emphasis than Sir Donald appears to give it.[1]   I should regret to give the impression that I thought inflation in the rest of the world was the *only* cause of the post-war dollar problem; of course there were vast structural changes, changes in relative prices of manufactures and primary products, the dislocation of war and post-war reconstruction, which in the early years at least would have given rise to severe difficulties.   But the fact remains that these difficulties were immensely magnified by loose financial policies and that, long after they should have been on the way to satisfactory solution, inflation where it persisted tended to prolong the agony.   And if it be true, as Sir Donald suggests, that, in future, prices in the rest of the world 'may well tend' on average to rise 1-2 per cent per annum faster than in the U.S., then the likelihood of recurrent dollar shortages in the future would seem to be established.   If we cannot learn more self-control than that, then we've had it.

### III

Sir Donald's emphasis, however, is somewhat different. The greater part of his text is taken up with an examination of the probability of dollar shortage even if deflation in the U.S. or inflation elsewhere is avoided.   He examines at great length possible trends in U.S. imports and exports of food, raw materials, and manufactures.   He discusses tourism, shipping, and investment.   And, as a result of all this, he concludes that 'at one extreme, the rest of the world's balance might tend to improve, but probably by an annual amount equivalent to less than 1 per cent of the trade in one direction between the two areas.   At the other extreme, the rest of the world's balance might tend to deteriorate by an annual amount equivalent to perhaps 3-4 per cent of this trade' (p. 285).   Perhaps it is wrong to infer from the physical space given to this investigation an order of intellectual perspective — statistical enquiries of this sort tend inevitably to run to length — and if so, I apologize in advance

---

[1] A fuller analysis of this episode from my point of view will be found in chapter iii of my *Economist in the Twentieth Century*.

to Sir Donald. But I am pretty sure that the majority of his readers will infer that it is this set of possibilities which is really worrying him.

Let me say at once that I have no objection to Sir Donald's figures as possibilities. I will confess to the philistine belief that, in fact, the most careful extrapolations of this kind are liable to be badly let down by the march of events. Fourteen years ago, when Sir Donald and I, in our respective rôles as public servants, were peering forward into the future of world trade with special reference to the reparation problem, what would either of us have said to anyone who predicted that by 1957, of all the nations of the free world save Switzerland, a Western Germany, bombed to pieces in war and ruthlessly hacked apart from her eastern provinces, would have the strongest currency and the best trading position? I have learned a great deal from Sir Donald's examination of possible alternatives; but my chief gain, I think, is an even deeper conviction than before that almost anything might happen.

Let us suppose, however, that Sir Donald's most pessimistic alternative were realized and that the fundamental conditions of supply and demand were to turn persistently against the rest of the world by an appreciable percentage year by year. Clearly, to restore equilibrium, adjustments of relative price levels would be necessary. Sir Donald does not recommend a floating rate; and, where key currencies are concerned, I think he is right. But since he does not think that, if the U.S. price level were to remain constant, the downward adjustments of price levels which would be necessary at a fixed rate would be either economically desirable or politically practicable, he prefers to contemplate occasional devaluations. He has not great confidence in the short-run effects of such measures, and for this reason he warns against the total dismantlement of the machinery of quantitative restriction and exchange control — he does not like it, he fears its cumulative effects if exclusive reliance is placed upon it, but he thinks that from time to time it may be necessary. But in the long run he thinks devaluation

works.  Unlike many writers on this subject who seem to
assume that all demand and supply curves have zero
elasticity, *i.e.* are utterly unresponsive to changes in price,
he believes that changes in relative prices and costs do
matter.  Indeed, it is in this way that a recurrent dollar
problem may at intervals be solved.

## IV

But is this really the best that we can hope for — assuming, that is to say, that the conditions of supply and demand
take an adverse turn?  I should have thought not.  The
fundamental *desideratum*, as Sir Donald's own analysis shows,
is a change in *relative* price and income levels ; and this can,
surely, be brought about by a rise in the U.S. just as much
as by a fall elsewhere.  In a world with a single money a
movement of this sort would be part of the equilibrating
mechanism.  If demand for the products of labour and
capital situated in one part increased in relation to demand
elsewhere, there would be a relative increase of incomes and
the prices of 'domestic' (*i.e.* locally produced) goods in that
quarter.  This would mean that the local workers and
property owners would be able to buy larger quantities of
goods and services elsewhere.  If the world money supply
were fixed, that would imply, other things being equal, some
rise in the quantity circulating in the area for whose products
demand had increased, and some diminution elsewhere.  If,
as it is more realistic to assume, the world money supply
were increasing, the same result could be obtained (and with
less friction) by some diversion of the increase where the
relative rise was needed, the supply elsewhere remaining
constant or not increasing so rapidly.

Why should we not hope for — or at least work for —
this sort of movement in the relations between the areas of a
non-unified world?  Why should we assume that adjustment
to changes in relative demand and supply must always take
place the more difficult way?  For reasons which I will
develop shortly, I do not think it is easy to secure the ideal

adjustments in a world of independent states.   But if we are
prepared to assume — as Sir Donald assumes for purposes
of this part of his analysis — that elsewhere there is no
inflation, why should we not assume that the U.S. authorities
will not allow the volume of expenditure to expand appropriately if their balance of payments is persistently favourable?
There is, of course, a danger that they may tend to regard
the objective of policy as attained if they only succeed in
keeping their own price level stable.   But I should certainly
not regard it as beyond reasonable or political possibility to
persuade them that on occasion the true interests of international stabilization required something a little more
complicated than that.

V

The real difficulty, I suspect, lies in the probability,
which Sir Donald has indicated earlier in his book, namely,
that elsewhere the general level of prices will rise faster than
in the U.S.   If the U.S. balance of payments is persistently
favourable *because of such influences*, there is indeed no reason
why there should be an internal financial expansion.   This
position is skies apart from the position we examined before.
There the favourable balance reflected a relative increase in
the value of U.S. production.   Here it reflects only an increase
in money or the velocity of circulation elsewhere.   There it
would be part of a movement of international equilibration.
Here it would be simply a spread of disequilibrating movements elsewhere.   Why should the U.S. import inflation?
The question would be asked;   and the answer must be that
there is no obligation.

The trouble goes very deep.   In the field of monetary
policy, as in so many other fields of policy, the existence
of independent sovereignties means the existence of independent policies;   and it is partly a matter of luck whether any
harmony exists.   In the last analysis, we shall not eliminate
the possibility of a dollar problem — or a sterling problem
or a mark problem — until in some way or other we have

gone much farther than we are at present towards financial unification of the free world, with a common clearing centre and a common central bank. I won't say that this is more probable than Sir Donald's recurrent catastrophies alleviated by makeshift expedients. But, taking a long view, I would not regard it as hopeless.

# THOUGHTS ON THE CRISIS OF 1957 [1]

## I

ONE of the many troubles about our present financial difficulties is the complexity of the intellectual issues involved.
To the superficial observer, at least, the crisis of last autumn
blew up in a comparatively clear sky : how many professional
prophets predicted anything like what actually happened ?
Moreover, even if, with wisdom after the event, we piece
together the various influences immediately operative, how
much agreement do we find concerning the longer-run
tendencies operative ? Was the inflation of the demand-pull
or the cost-push variety ? To what extent is the trouble to
be attributed to the deficiencies of monetary policy as an
instrument or is it true to say that the instrument had not
been appropriately applied ? These and such-like questions
beset any attempt at diagnosis of the crisis.

When we turn to prescription, the position is no less complicated. Was a 7 per cent Bank Rate justified as a crisis
measure or was it simply the last resort of a conventional
misapprehension of the situation ? Is a ceiling on advances
an appropriate control of the volume of money ? Was there
no alternative to cuts in investment ? How are all these
measures to be conceived in relation to developments in the
outside world ? And in any case where do we go from here ?
Is inflation really an evil and, if so, how far are we prepared
to go to stop it ? Is a centrally controlled wages policy an
appropriate remedy ? What should be our attitude to the
question of the reserve ? It is to problems of this sort that
we need at least a provisional answer before we can make up
our minds on even the smaller issues of day-to-day policy.
Small wonder that at the present time there is more con-

[1] A paper originally published in *Lloyds Bank Review* for April 1958.

fusion, more division among men of knowledge and good-will than perhaps at any time in post-war history.

It is not my belief that I know all the right answers to these tremendous questions. Anyone who has participated continuously in public discussion of such matters over any long period of time — in my case, more than twenty-five years — must, if he is candid, admit to many occasions on which he has made mistakes and the strong probability that he may make other mistakes in the future. We are all in the same boat in this respect. But if we are to make any progress at all we must go on exchanging opinions and seeking to set forth, with mutual respect and toleration of other points of view — commodities in somewhat short supply in certain quarters recently — the ultimate reasons for our own atti-tudes. At any rate, it is in the hope that in this way we may eventually come to greater agreement that I venture to offer these very fragmentary and very imperfect reflections.

## II

Let me begin with the immediate causes of the crisis.

The first point which deserves to be made is a negative one : this was *not* a crisis of the current account. Despite the embarrassments of the ill-conceived Suez adventure, in the first half-year we were running a surplus on balance-of-payments account at the rate of £250 millions per annum ; and the indications are that for the full year the surplus was probably of the order of £200 millions. The belief that it was the trade figures which were to blame was ill-founded. It is true that a surplus of £200 millions per annum is not all that might be wished. If we are to play our part in overseas development and, at the same time, achieve a reinforcement of the reserves commensurate with our external obligations, something more like £450 to £500 millions is desirable. Still, the fact that it fell short of the ideal does not turn a quite respectable surplus into an alarming deficit. The true causes of the trouble have to be looked for in quite a different direction.

There can be no doubt that for some time prior to the crisis the position of sterling in the foreign exchange markets had been under some suspicion and the holders of sterling had been apt to be apprehensive of the slightest adverse movement. It is probable, however, that the immediate occasion for the beginning of the run was the partial devaluation of the franc which, perhaps because it was only partial, inevitably gave rise to expectations of further changes. There were rumours of an upward revaluation of the mark and all sorts of vague talk of a general realignment of European currencies.

In such circumstances it was only to be expected that sterling should come under pressure. There was no likelihood that sterling would appreciate in any such realignment and some possibility, to put it mildly, that it would depreciate in terms of the stronger currencies, the mark and the Swiss franc. Now, whatever may be the moral obligations of British nationals when confronting such prospects, there is obviously no obligation on foreigners to expose their funds to loss or to forgo the opportunity of gain. Some movement out of sterling was, therefore, almost inevitable.

In the general position of London ever since the war, such movements tend to have a snowball tendency. The reserves are so small in relation to our external liabilities that, if there is a significant downward movement, all sorts of holders, who would not normally have wished to move, begin to think that perhaps it would be better to get out before things get very much worse. This mood tends to spread. Creditors, who have payments due to them in sterling, withdraw their money earlier than would otherwise have been the case. Debtors, who have payments to make, defer payment as long as they can in the hope that it will cost them less in the end. Pure speculation begins to play its part and extensive bear positions are created. If the reserves were larger, the danger of this kind of development would be to that extent less. With a really adequate reserve, the capital account could sustain substantial withdrawals without the danger of a run.

But, even with the reserves at such a low level as ours since the war, the situation is not necessarily unmanageable. There is room for much difference of opinion concerning the policies adopted last autumn. But one thing certainly has been demonstrated: that a run of the kind which was taking place can be stopped, if sufficiently strong action be taken. And if action is taken sufficiently soon, and if there exists a general expectation that it will be carried to any lengths requisite to reverse the drain, then, as likely as not, very severe action will not be necessary. This is not a universal rule. It is not difficult to think of external drains which could not be dealt with in this manner. But in general it is true that, where there exists general confidence in the determination of the authorities concerned to adopt the policies necessary to safeguard whatever reserve there is, there a cumulative deterioration of the situation is unlikely.

This takes us to the very heart of the trouble last year. Rightly or wrongly, there was no confidence. There was no confidence in the willingness of the financial authorities to take action to safeguard the reserve. And, more fundamentally, there was no confidence in the willingness of the government to pursue policies which would mean that the reserve was not continually in danger. As we have seen already, it was not true that the current account was in any immediate danger. But it was true that it was feared very generally that policies were dominant which would bring just this danger about. The failure to restore a position which had begun to deteriorate two years earlier, the continuation of inflation and the prospect of rising levels of public expenditure, all contrived to produce an expectation of further deterioration. And when such expectations are prevalent they tend to bring their own realization.

Thus, while the immediate occasion of our troubles last autumn was provided by external events not within our immediate control, the cause of their magnification and the apparent unmanageability of the situation was a general belief in the weakness of our own internal policy. It would certainly be wrong to argue that, if there had been no internal weakness, there would have been no alarms and excursions regarding France and Germany. But if the internal position had been strong, these alarms and excursions would have been very much easier to deal with. And the root cause of our weakness, of our failure to accumulate a sufficient reserve and to achieve a position in international trade strong enough to be immune to the impact of international rumour, was the continuation of internal inflation.

It is, therefore, to the examination of this situation that we must now turn.

### III

Let us begin by reminding ourselves of what had actually happened. If 1950 be taken as 100, by the autumn of 1957 the cost-of-living index had risen to 143. This shows an average rise of nearly 6·5 per cent per annum. During the same period in Germany, prices rose to 115, or by 2·2 per cent per annum, and in the United States to 118, or by 2·7 per cent per annum. Nor was there any pronounced tendency for this movement to cease. Since early in 1955 various measures of restraint, including a credit squeeze of sorts, had been in operation. Yet in the twelve months from August 1956, to August 1957, the rise in prices was still as much as 4 per cent. The fact that, with a rate of inflation so substantially higher than in the two other great industrial countries mentioned, our balance of payments was not in a much poorer condition, must indicate a very considerable degree of under-valuation in 1949 when the sterling parity was altered. But, obviously, such elbow room has its limits. It was not unreasonable, therefore, for both foreign speculators and observers nearer home to feel that, if the inflation continued in this manner (*i.e.* at a greater rate than elsewhere), then there was grave trouble ahead.

What was the prime cause of this tendency? Did it arise on the side of demand or on the side of costs? If it was a demand inflation, the operative factors were an urge to business expansion born of the prospect of good profits, a situation in which liquid funds were plentifully available to business, either in their own reserves or in capital markets where the terms of borrowing were very much lower than the prospects of profits. If, on the other hand, the upward pressure on prices is conceived to have originated on the side of costs, the significant factors in the situation would have been a continued pressure of the trade unions to better their relative position, and it would have been a continued rise in wage-rates which, in spite of apprehensions of diminished profits, compelled producers continually to raise their prices.[1] Clearly, both explanations are conceivable. The question is, which fits the facts?

From my point of view, for the greater part of the post-war period it is the explanation in terms of the pull of demand which has the greater plausibility. If the prime movement had been on the side of costs, the prospect of profits would have been continually threatened, the index of wage-rates would have tended to rise faster than the index of weekly wage earnings, the volume of vacancies would have tended to fall below the level of applications. And these things did not happen. For the greater part of the time, profit prospects were good, earnings were rising faster than wage-rates, and the volume of vacancies remained higher than the volume of applications. As I see the picture, the rise of wage-rates was, for the most part, the *consequence* rather than the *cause* of the situation. The demand for labour was so strong that, even if the trade unions had been much weaker, it is probable that a similar movement would have taken place. Indeed, paradoxically enough, it might have been more accentuated: the cumbersome process of collective bargaining tends to take longer than the operations of freer markets.

Towards the end of the period and at the present time the picture tends to change. It is probably true to say that, when you put the brake on a demand inflation you are

[1] For a fuller account of the possibility and the *modus operandi* of cost inflation see my paper on 'Full Employment as an Objective', reprinted in *The Economist in the Twentieth Century*. In the light of this paper, written shortly after the war, I confess I find slightly surprising suggestions that I am unaware of the dangers of cost inflation.

then confronted with the danger of a cost inflation. If the trade unions have got into the habit of cashing in on the demand inflation every spring, then very naturally they will tend to go on trying to do so for a time even though the increase of demand has slackened. They will continue to press for increased wage-rates; and now, if inflation proceeds, it can be described as having its origin on the side of costs.

This explanation also seems to me to fit the facts of recent history. The penultimate phase of the U.K. inflation begins in 1954 with the lowering of discount rates and various budgetary easements, notably the change in investment allowances. An investment boom of full dimensions develops. Then in 1955 sundry checks begin to be applied, the first credit squeeze, the autumn budget, and so on; and the prospects of profit, although still pretty good, become less attractive, the disparity between the rise of earnings and wage-rates begins to diminish, the gap between vacancies and applications narrows. . . . Inflation from the pull of demand tends to diminish. Inflation from the push of costs becomes more likely.

All this is obviously very controversial: there are many observers of the situation, whose judgment I respect, who would differ considerably in emphasis, giving more weight throughout to the push of costs, less to the pull of demand, than I find appropriate. But on one point I hope we should all be agreed; namely, *that none of this could happen if there was a sufficiently strong control of the supply of money* (i.e. *cash plus bank deposits*). By this I do not wish to beg the question whether such a control is itself desirable — there will be much more to say about that later on. Nor do I argue in the least that the supply of money is the *only* factor governing the volume of expenditure: it is almost humiliating at this time of day to have to insist that any form of the quantity theory held by any reputable economist in the last two hundred years has taken account of the demand for money (expressing itself *via* velocity) as well as of the supply thereof. All that is contended is that, if the supply of money is adequately varied, the other influences on expenditure can be offset so as to prevent inflation.

But if this is so, how did it come about that in all these years the inflation was allowed to continue? It cannot be argued, at any rate since the return of the Conservative government in 1951, that the authorities were opposed to the use of monetary policy *per se*. In the early years after the war, under the Labour government, this may have been so : at any rate a positive monetary policy was not pursued. But since 1951 all that was supposed to have been changed : the return to monetary policy was claimed as one of the positive achievements of the change of régime. And, in the first crisis of that period, monetary policy had indeed some effect. Yet inflation reasserted itself, and when, since the summer of 1955, there was some show of control by way of monetary policy, the results, at least until the drastic measures of last autumn, were not all that might have been wished. It would be going much too far to say that the credit squeeze and the other monetary measures which accompanied it had *no* effect — a case could be made out for the view that by the winter of 1956–57 they were beginning to work. But it is quite obvious that up to last autumn they had not stopped the inflation.

At least three reasons can be given for these disappointing developments.

In the first place come the deficiencies of fiscal policy. The budgets of 1954 and 1955, with their changes in investment allowances and tax reductions, definitely tended to an increase of general expenditure. And thenceforward, until the Thorneycroft budget of 1957, it must be noted that very little was done to bring the surplus above the line into a non-inflationary relation with the below-the-line deficit.

Now, monetary policy, properly conceived and executed, can be a very powerful means of stopping an inflation. But if fiscal policy is tending the other way, then the strain put upon monetary policy is to that extent greater : even tighter conditions are required. And that, clearly, was one of the governing circumstances. With their fiscal measures — or lack of measures — successive Chancellors tended to undo what they were trying to do with the discount rate and credit policy generally. It is easy enough to understand and indeed to sympathize with the motives. The long-run arguments in favour of reduction of some taxes are very strong indeed. But reductions of taxation, unless accompanied by reductions of expenditure or by the substitution of other taxes, are apt to have an inflationary influence. And this is one of the things which has been happening since 1954.

Secondly, given the task to be accomplished, then, even on the assumption that the machine was in good working order — an assumption to be questioned in a moment — it seems clear to me that what monetary measures were adopted were both too little and too late. The theory of monetary policy does not say that *any* raising of interest rates, *any* tightening of the credit base, is sufficient to curb overall expenditure, however strongly it is developing: it says that *some* level of interest rates, *some* curtailment of the credit basis may be relied upon to have that effect. And what these critical levels are varies obviously with the general tendencies of the system, and the time of the operation. A small touch on the brakes at an early stage may be more effective than greater pressure later on. If there is an overall budgetary deficit, then the optimal level of interest rates will be higher than if there were an overall budget surplus.

But here too the evolution of policy was the reverse of what was required. At the time of the budgetary easements in 1954, interest rates had recently been lowered. Throughout the ensuing months, as the inflation gathered strength, monetary policy was further eased. Then, when rates were eventually moved up, the movement was so small that, even if the machine had been working properly, it would have been very surprising if it had been effective.[1] At each stage, when change came it seemed to be wrung out of the authorities long after outside opinion had formed the conclusion that it was necessary. Clearly, this is a matter on which

---

[1] With prices rising at the rate at which they rose in those years, real, as distinct from money, rates of interest were not far from zero — or less.

there can be much argument in detail. But I do not think it unfair to say that, until the autumn of last year, nothing that was done in this sphere gave the impression that it was likely to succeed.

All this, I suspect, would be true even if, as I have assumed hitherto, the machinery of control had been working as it is supposed to work in the standard textbooks — if, that is to say, the Bank of England, through its discount rate and its open market operations, had had effective control of the volume of credit. This brings us to the third reason for failure.

For, in fact, it is now pretty clear that the control was no longer working according to the standard model. It has been demonstrated by Professor Sayers [1] and by the editor of this journal [2] that the immense volume of floating debt now outstanding introduces a complication into the situation which is not dealt with in the textbooks. To all intents and purposes the Treasury bill has become the equivalent of money, and, with the Treasury bill issue in other hands, the control of the credit base by the central bank is necessarily weakened. The application of the lever no longer automatically applies the brake. A detailed explanation of the events of recent years in these terms is still a matter of considerable obscurity: only the Bank of England is in full possession of the necessary information — and that information has never yet been made public. But, speaking broadly, it is clear enough that in recent years there have been times when, because of government borrowings on short term, the Bank has no longer been in a position to control the situation. At a time when too exclusive a reliance was being placed upon monetary policy, the apparatus thereof was defective. The braking mechanism, so to speak, was in continual danger of failing to grip. And on several occasions it did fail.

But this brings us to the events of last autumn.

[1] *Central Banking after Bagehot*, pp. 92-107. 'The Determination of the Volume of Bank Deposits: England 1955–6.'
[2] *Lloyds Bank Review*, April 1956, pp. 24-38. 'The Floating Debt Problem.'

## IV

Memories tend to fade of events which were unpleasant. To see what happened in proper perspective it is desirable to remind ourselves of the situation with which we were confronted.

The central fact of this situation was the drain of reserves. For many weeks before September 19th, gold and dollars had been pouring out of the country at a rate rising to £100 millions a month. At the lowest point of the crisis the reserve had fallen to $1850 millions. That is to say, at the then rate of withdrawal, there would have been a total exhaustion within a matter of months. But, of course, long before this, as the process proceeded, the rate would have increased: there would have developed a veritable *sauve qui peut*. The plain fact was that, if nothing had been done, either devaluation or a repudiation of current obligations was a virtual certainty within a few weeks.

Now, it is a matter of fairly general agreement that, if there is what the Bretton Woods statutes call a 'fundamental disequilibrium' in the external relations of a financial centre, then devaluation may be an appropriate remedy. If prices and costs in any area have got so out of line with prices and costs elsewhere that, to restore equilibrium at fixed rates of exchange, a general deflation of local rates of pay would be necessary, then it is better to alter the rates of exchange. This is true whether the disequilibrium is due to deflation elsewhere or to inflation at home. If deflation elsewhere is the cause, there is not much occasion for argument: there is no reason to import deflation. But the same is true if domestic inflation has been the culprit. Inflation of this sort is an evil: but so too is deflation. Rather than endure the damages of long drawn-out unemployment and loss of production, better operate on the foreign exchanges.

But the crisis last autumn was not a crisis of this nature. As we have seen already, it was not a crisis on the current account. It was the capital account which was in difficulties. And here the trouble was due to a fear of devaluation or a fear that further inflation would upset the current account and so make devaluation necessary.

In such circumstances it would probably be more or less generally agreed that devaluation would have been totally inappropriate. It would have robbed our creditors. It would have made our imports more expensive. It would have strengthened the tendencies to internal inflation. It was, therefore, entirely inadvisable as a voluntary policy; and to have sat still doing nothing and watching devaluation forced upon us would have been an abject failure of government.

For similar reasons, I cannot believe that on this occasion any good purpose could have been served by letting the rate float. The policy of the floating rate is an acutely controversial matter and it would be idle to claim that there is any general consensus of opinion about it. But I think that it would be generally agreed that a moment of extreme weakness is not the moment for making such an experiment. The rate would certainly have plunged downwards, precipitating further withdrawals and, in the absence of countervailing measures, provoking further internal inflation, eventually justifying a permanently lower rate — the so-called ratchet effect. Although in general I prefer the system of fixed rates with the possibility of agreed adjustment à la Bretton Woods, I would not rule out the use of the floating rate on any possible occasion: a depression of the 1929 intensity in the U.S. might well create a situation in which for a time it was advisable to let the rate take the strain. But the situation in September last year was not at all like this and, in my judgment, a floating rate would only have made things worse.

As for the repudiation of current obligations which would have been involved by the re-imposition of full exchange control and the blocking of the sterling balances, surely it would have been both dishonourable and inexpedient. It would have been dishonourable since these balances have been left here on the definite understanding that they would be available whenever required. In the years immediately after the war there was a case, which I, for one, thought very cogent, for imposing some restraint on the release of the abnormal accumulations of wartime. But that is ancient history: for the most part, the wartime balances have been run down; the present balances have been deposited since then. To close down on them without putting up a fight would be the most flagrant failure to keep faith with our clients. It would be inexpedient too: whatever we may think of the eventual future of the sterling area, whether we foresee for it a glorious future or whether we think it will eventually give way to other arrangements, we surely do not wish to see it liquidated overnight with all that that would imply. But that is what the blocking of balances and the re-imposition of all-over exchange control would involve.

But if all these courses were rejected, what remained? In my judgment, at least, the course which was actually adopted: a clear announcement that the rate of exchange was not to be changed, backed up by the announcement of measures which should prove unmistakably to the world at large that the inflation was not to be allowed to continue.

The formula is simple enough. But there can be no doubt that its application involved greater hazards than would have been present earlier on. It is safe to say that, up to last summer, at almost any time in the preceding six years, the government could have stopped the inflation without running any risks that really mattered. To stop a small local inflation when the rest of the world economy is running at a high level involves no danger of subsequent deflation. But again and again we refused to grasp the nettle. With an unemployment percentage continually lower than anything recorded in our peacetime history, we let fears of totally imaginary dangers inhibit the very mild measures that would have been necessary. But now the position was beginning to change. A recession was developing in the United States. Should we not be imposing our anti-inflationary measures at a time when there was at least a risk that anti-deflationary measures would become necessary a little later on?

As I see things, the danger was — and is — a real one.

The possibility of a deepening of the U.S. recession was not imaginary. But neither was the possibility of a total collapse of sterling. And the one danger was certain and near at hand, while the other was still remote and conjectural. Moreover, it is difficult to believe that, if our crisis had been allowed to intensify with an eventual immobilization of the reserves and free funds of the sterling area, there would have been any substantial alleviation of the troubles of the world at large — quite the contrary indeed. Hence the common-sense maxim of dealing with dangers one at a time as they materialized was still applicable. The order of the day was to save the pound. If there was a world depression by next summer and the pound had been saved, perhaps we could do something to help. But if the pound had collapsed and London was immobilized in the splints and bandages of a post-crisis exchange control, that would be out of the question. In such circumstances, to refuse to stop our own inflation because later on deflation might come elsewhere would seem to be about as sensible as refusing, when the house is on fire, to call the fire engine on the ground that there may be floods later on.

V

Now for a few brief comments on the measures actually adopted — the raising of the Bank Rate and the limitations on advances and expenditure. I will also add a word on the absence of any further limitations on consumption.

(a) *The Raising of the Bank Rate*

To begin with the Bank Rate. From my point of view the surprising thing about this episode is, not that it happened but rather that so many people were surprised that it happened — and among these, not merely everyday citizens, to whom the proceedings of a great capital market are perhaps inevitably always something of a mystery, but also professional dealers whose livelihood depends upon an intelligent understanding of these matters. I am sure that an observer from Mars who, before his visit, had worked up his knowledge of mundane financial crises by a short study of how the majority of central banks have behaved in the majority of past financial crises, would not have been at all surprised. Yet here were people who had been in the business all their lives to whom the bare possibility does not seem ever to have occurred. No wonder they were a little upset.

Now, it may be admitted at once that the effectiveness of movements of the Bank Rate as a sole means for controlling the total volume of expenditure may very justly be called in question. It is certainly arguable, as I have argued above, that the powers of the Bank in our own time have been gravely impaired by a distended volume of short-term government debt, and that, for that reason, an effective control of the money supply demands more drastic and comprehensive measures. There will be a good deal to say about this later on.

But this is not to say that, as a crisis measure, a raising of the Bank Rate is to be regarded as ineffective. It is, of course, not true that such a movement, carrying with it, as it does, a corresponding movement of conventional rates on borrowing and lending, not to mention strong psychological effects on the security markets, has *no* effect on the volume of internal expenditure — even though it be arguable that such effects can be as well produced by other less expensive means. And, internal effects apart, it would surely be quite absurd to argue that it has no effect on the movement of funds into and out of the country. It has a direct effect *via* the cash incentive : it increases the advantages of leaving money here or bringing it in ; it diminishes the relative attraction of other places. The indirect effect is even more important : it is a signal to all and sundry that the integrity of the currency is to be preserved. Whatever the deficiencies of our present machinery, it is an important fact that the members of other financial centres tend to regard the movement of money rates as an index of policy. To them the raising of the Bank Rate here is a sign that the pound is to be defended.

I wonder how many of those who have been most critical since this measure was taken in fact would have been prepared at such a moment to forgo these advantages. With gold and dollars pouring out at catastrophic rates, would it not have been just a trifle purist to have abstained from the use of an instrument which again and again in the past had been proved to have the effect of arresting this kind of drain? I do not think many of the critics would have wanted to devalue. Some, perhaps, would have argued for complete exchange control, though it is doubtful if at the same time they would have welcomed the consequences of such a régime — a complete break-up of the sterling area. But, if such expedients were not acceptable, it is not easy to see any practical alternative to what was actually done. Or is it to be argued that the drain would have come to an end of its own accord — as the result of speeches by ministers assuring the world at large that in fact everything in the garden was lovely?

## (b) *The Limitation on Advances*

If this argument is correct, Bank Rate is still an indispensable weapon for dealing with an acute crisis. For dealing with a secular tendency to inflation, however, it is not a particularly suitable instrument. For this purpose it is desirable to adopt other measures for limiting the flow of expenditure.

So far as the banking system was concerned, the measure which was actually adopted was the imposition of an upper limit on the aggregate of advances. Each of the clearing banks undertook not to exceed in the present twelve months the average level of its advances in the preceding year. There were small modifications of detail for particular lines of credit. But this in substance was the broad policy adopted.

Now, conceived as a crisis measure, to be adopted at short notice with the minimum of resistance from all immediately concerned, there is probably a good deal to be said for this device. It has precedents in past policies. It requires no legislation or statutory regulations. And, despite the strictures which I shall develop shortly, it cannot be said to be without effect; there would not be so much grumbling if this were in fact the case.

Nevertheless, conceived as a policy for the longer period, still more if conceived as an expedient to be adopted whenever this kind of danger emerges, it is open to considerable criticism. It bears unequally upon different banks, according to the different lending policies which they have been pursuing. It tends to paralyse financial competition, which in the long run must be a very bad thing. And, as a partial control, it does not really go to the root of the matter. The root of the matter is control of expenditure as a whole.

But to do this the fundamental desideratum is control of the supply of money. Given overall control at that end, there can be adaptation to all sorts of vagaries of expenditure in particular sectors. Given an absence of such control, there can be no guarantee that control in one sector will not be frustrated by the absence of control elsewhere. This is not to say that, even if the supply of money is under control, there may not arise a need for supplementary special controls. But it is to say that, if it is not under control, the whole system is liable to get out of hand.

Now, as already emphasized, the disquieting feature of the recent situation was that the money supply was not under effective control: the excessive volume of short-term debt has weakened the hand of the central bank. The monetization of debt has made the Treasury rather than the Bank of England the arbiter of the total volume of cash plus deposits. The needs of short-term borrowing rather than the needs of the system for cash and credit have been liable to disturb overall stability.

In more normal circumstances the appropriate remedy for such a situation would be funding. The volume of Treasury bills should be reduced until there is no threat to the complete control of the credit base by the Bank of England. It is true that this would involve some increase in the annual debt charge. But to keep this charge down by techniques which endanger the future of the pound is not sensible policy. An increase would be a small price to pay to regain control of the credit base and hence of aggregate demand in general.

Unfortunately, in a financial crisis such operations are not necessarily practicable. Throughout the greater part of the year the position had been becoming more difficult in this respect. After years of passive acquiescence in lending in a deteriorating standard of value, the investor had gradually become aware of what was happening and was demanding progressively higher returns on fixed interest securities. The Church of England and the learned societies had led the way; and now the man in the street had tumbled to the fact that if you lend for a money return of 4 per cent per annum net and the value of money is falling at the same rate, then you are lending at a zero rate of interest. The run on the pound intensified the difficulty. It is safe to say that, in August and September of last year, orthodox funding on a scale necessary to re-establish control of the credit base would have been quite out of the question.

In such an emergency there seems to me strong argument for some extraordinary measure which, by operating on the liquidity position of the banking system, shall impose limits on its total lending. If action can be taken at this end, then there need be no paralysis of competition, no wooden interference with different modes of doing business. But the credit base as a whole can be brought under effective control.

In public discussion, the device most favoured for accomplishing this has been compulsory variation of minimum liquidity ratios. On the assumption that, in modern conditions, it is the liquidity position, rather than the cash reserve, which ultimately governs the supply of money, it is argued that powers should be taken to require the observance of minimum liquidity ratios and that these ratios should be varied according to the requirements of general policy. This is not the same as the existing provision of the banking law

183

in the U.S. under which the Federal Reserve Board has the power to vary minimum cash reserve requirements; although it has sometimes been mistaken for this, it is a more comprehensive requirement. But it is a device of the same type conceived in relation to the exigencies of our own system.

In principle, there seems little objection to such a regulation provided it is regarded as an emergency expedient. But there are technical difficulties which are often overlooked. The actual liquidity position of the banks varies from week to week, and, since the effects on investments and advances of such changes are multiple, it would be necessary to make very frequent changes in the prescribed ratio. Moreover, these changes would have to be by small fractions, not easy to judge and not easy to justify to the public.

Much superior in my judgment is the plan which was recommended as far back as August 1956, by Messrs. Paish and Alford [1] and again by Messrs. Alford and Edey as the crisis was developing,[2] namely, the imposition of a fixed liquidity ratio — or one varied at comparatively long intervals — plus a revival, for the duration of the crisis, of the system of Treasury Deposit Receipts (T.D.R.s) whereby the banks are required from week to week to keep an appropriately varying volume of assets in a form which is definitely illiquid. Such a method is capable of doing all that is claimed for the system of variable liquidity ratios but with much greater refinement and precision. The appropriate variations in the supply of money are now secured *via* the variations in the volume of T.D.R.s rather than the variation of the liquidity ratio. The principle of the operation is the same.

Let me hasten to add that, in my judgment, in being regimented in this manner, the banks would have a real grievance. Their business would be being interfered with because of a situation created not by their policy but by the policy, or rather lack of policy, of the government. But I do not believe that this kind of interference would be more

---

[1] 'How Interest Rates cut Spending', *The Banker*, vol. lvi, no. 367, pp. 476-87.      [2] *London and Cambridge Economic Bulletin*, September 1957.

damaging to their business than the interference to which they are now subjected under the present arrangements of the credit squeeze; and if there were some definite understanding that the regulation was to be regarded definitely as transitory, to be relinquished as soon as orthodox funding on an adequate scale was once more practicable, I do not think that the grievance would be intolerable.

It may well be that the occasion for this sort of thing is even now passing. As the prospect of inflation wanes, the possibilities of orthodox funding become more extensive. Nevertheless, it seems to me that there is perhaps some utility in thus spelling out the principles of alternative measures even if on this occasion they prove to be no longer applicable.

(c) *The Limitations on Expenditure*

Finally, we may note the proposed limitations on expenditure.

This is so political a subject that it is not easy to say much about it that is not right outside the sphere of economics in any sense whatever. How much the country will stand in the shape of reduction here; what it would be prudent politically to exempt there; to what extent discredit will arise if a gesture is not made in this direction — these are not questions on which the economist who does not care to transform himself into Adam Smith's 'crafty and insidious animal', the politician, has very much to say. Two comments, however, are perhaps permissible.

The first is that, in the context of what was actually proposed, the term reduction is misleading. The celebrated 'cuts' were prospective. Extra expenditure which had been projected was to be forgone. Doubtless, this was very important. Increases on the scale which had been contemplated would have imposed still more strain on the system, and we must not underestimate the political effort apparently necessary to impose even this degree of restraint. Nevertheless, if we are to use words accurately, not *reduction* but *standstill* was the more appropriate description.

The second comment is that, in the subsequent discussion, the nature of the margin for manœuvre has been often misconceived. To judge from leading articles and correspondence in the Press, it would appear that there were immense savings available if only ministers would order a naturally spendthrift and wasteful public service to be more careful all round. But this is a pathetic and dangerous delusion. Doubtless there is always a little waste even in the best regulated establishments; and perhaps there are a few hundred thousands to be gained by general cheese-paring on small items which are unable to defend themselves and which, on intrinsic merits, perhaps even deserve some increase. But all the main reductions possible involve, not administrative, but political decisions, and major decisions at that; and decisions on matters of this sort are the decisions which most ministers of most parties tend to shirk. Perhaps they are right. Perhaps some wisdom, invisible to those not in the fray, prevents them from steps which would disintegrate, not only their own peace of mind, but also the fabric of society. But if this is so, then standstill, or a slower creep forward, is the most we can hope for in the sphere of public expenditure; and in respect of what has been done recently we should be grateful for small mercies.

## (d) *The Absence of Limitations on Consumption*

The criticism is sometimes made of the measures adopted last autumn that their main incidence fell almost wholly on investment. The raising of the Bank Rate, the ceiling on advances, and the 'cuts' in public expenditure all tended to have their main effect, directly at least, by restraints on the volume of investment.

The immediate answer to this, I suppose, is that, in an inflationary situation, the cutting of investment is the cutting of investment for which no corresponding savings were planned. If the disposition to save had been adequate, then there would have been no danger of inflation.

Nevertheless, in a situation in which so much is artificial, I see no particular reason to believe that the existing volume of savings is, in any sense, optimal; and I see no objection in principle to applying restraints on consumption in order to ease inflationary pressure. If, in such a situation, there were available tax variations which, without damaging the incentive to work or to save, could have restrained pressure at the consumption end, then in my judgment there would be good ground for imposing them.

The trouble is to discover appropriate and practical methods — particularly when the crisis blows up in an inter-budgetary period. I confess that I see no good grounds for still further variations in a purchase tax system which is already sufficiently arbitrary and discriminatory. If there existed a general sales tax in its place — still more, if there existed a general sales tax *plus* general exemption allowance [1] such as has been proposed by Professor Paish — I would say that the circumstances of last autumn provided a copy-book case for the use of variations both of the rate and the exemption allowance, as counter-inflationary influences. Unfortunately, such expedients do not exist and it is not possible to improvise them overnight.

Equally efficacious, and perhaps politically no more difficult to impose, would be variations in the contributions of employers and employed to the social insurance funds. This plan, invented by Professor Meade, was blessed by both parties in the Coalition White Paper on Employment Policy. After the war, the essential machinery was actually built into social insurance legislation by the Labour government, and there can be no doubt in principle that comparatively small variations here could have powerful countervailing influence either against inflation or deflation. Unfortunately, the machinery was never used by those who installed it, and probably, at the present time, there is a good deal of political and administrative dust in the works. I still think, however, that it is a very good plan and that on some future occasion it should be tried — either one way or the other.

[1] To be effected by a distribution of coupons entitling each citizen to a certain volume of tax-free purchases.

## VI

And now what? There can be no question that, whether or not they were the best that could be conceived, the measures actually adopted last autumn have stopped the run. Since September 19th the reserves have been mounting again — not perhaps quite as rapidly as might have been hoped, but nevertheless unmistakably and strongly upward. There have been various signs that confidence is not completely re-established — the downward flicker following the very hostile reception of the Cohen Report, for instance — and the prospect of divided counsels and political dissension in the future gives rise to legitimate apprehension. But, for the moment, the atmosphere of crisis has passed and we can look round a little.

The first question which naturally arises is how we now stand in relation to developments in America. Has the contraction there reached a point which is so liable to infect us with similar tendencies as to warrant a complete reversal of policy here? Are we confronted with a major depression in the world at large against which it is a prime necessity for us to take independent internal action?

The enquiry is serious, and, as I have indicated already, I think that it deserves to be taken seriously. I should, therefore, like to make it quite clear that it is my view that if the contraction in the U.S. were to assume the dimensions of a major depression, it would be incumbent upon us to adopt insulating measures. I do not think that this would be at all easy; it is quite possible that present rates of exchange would have to be sacrificed in the process. But it seems to me plain that, in the event of such a development, such policies would be necessary.

If, however, this does not happen; if the American contraction is arrested before it goes into something really severe, then I think any attempt on our part to take the initiative would not only be premature but also dangerous. The pound is certainly not yet strong enough to risk the impression of a renewal of inflation. Anything which tended now to raise our prices and costs while the rest of the world was consolidating at a lower level would be a renewed embarrassment. And from the point of view of the world at large, we should certainly do no one a good service by a policy which once more threatened the position of sterling. Clearly, we must avoid unnecessary severity. The object of the present exercise is to strengthen the pound and prevent expenditure rising faster than productivity, and, as the danger to the capital account diminishes, there will be no need to prolong measures which were specifically suitable for dealing with that particular difficulty. But to go beyond such relaxations would be risky. This is very unfortunate. It would be very gratifying to be in a position in which we could afford to take the initiative in stimulating a world revival. But to be able to do that now we should have put our position in order earlier. With a strong reserve all sorts of things would have been possible that with a weak reserve are a source of peril.

Now, I do not profess to know what is going to happen in America. Where expert opinion on the spot is so sorely divided, it is surely to set a high value on one's powers as a prophet to pretend to predict from a distance. I confess I find it hard to believe that, in an election year with so many shots in the locker, the Administration and Congress will be content to witness a dangerous deterioration. But such things have happened before and I would not be sure. What seems to me to be fairly clear is that there have been no developments yet which, in our special and highly peculiar position, would call for extraordinary action. I hope myself that the U.S. Administration will redouble its efforts to put the gears in reverse : I wish, for our sake, that they had done so earlier. But I see no immediate call for such action here. The situation calls for unceasing vigilance, and if things get very much worse we may find ourselves the other side of the looking-glass where all sorts of rules are reversed. But so far I do not think this has happened. For us at least — although not, I suspect, for the U.S. — the maxims of prudence still have a positive sign.

Assuming this to be correct, let us enquire a little further concerning the nature of these maxims. Assuming that events elsewhere do not compel a drastic change, how should we wish our own development to proceed? What are the fundamental objectives of policy in regard to expenditure and the price level?

It should be clear in the first place that these objectives do *not* include deflation — policies designed to produce a positive contraction of incomes or the price level. It should not be necessary to labour this point. But I am afraid that experience proves that it is. It has become almost a habit, recently, among certain writers and speakers, that if a man argues against *in*flation, he should be at once denounced for recommending *de*flation. I suppose that, in most cases at least, one ought to treat this as if it were sincere : the subject is difficult and tempers are easily aroused. But deflation is certainly not the only alternative to inflation. It is perfectly possible — and until recently I should have thought that it would have been assumed to be the most natural attitude — to be opposed to both and to regard some sort of overall stability as the objective. At any rate, despite popular oratory, I have yet to meet any responsible person who wishes to impose a positive deflation. To stop inflation, that is the objective; and to talk of deflation and mass unemployment, when the cost-of-living index has only just stopped rising and the unemployment percentage is still lower than in most other countries of the world and at most times in modern history, is simply to darken counsel.

But do we really want to stop inflation? I suppose there are very few politicians who would admit to wanting it to continue. But a great many act as if they were prepared to tolerate such an outcome; and there are certainly others, not so directly connected with politics, who are definitely prepared to argue as if it were something which we ought to put up with. In modern conditions, it is contended, while of course hyper-inflation is to be avoided, a creeping inflation is to be accepted as the condition most conducive to growth.

To make stable money the objective is to risk stagnation and unemployment.

I find this position unacceptable. I do not in the least deny that the process of *stopping* an inflation may involve some temporary check to production and employment: if you are swerving towards a precipice, some temporary slowing up is the price you have to pay for re-establishing a safer direction of motion. But I know no reason which would lead to the conclusion that smart rates of growth and high levels of employment are impossible on a steady price level. In the recent history of Germany, for instance, there is ample evidence disproving this view.

But suppose there are strong trade unions and an incessant pressure for wages rising faster than productivity, is not this expectation vitiated? Do there not then exist conditions in which growth can be sustained only at the expense of some degree of inflation?

The question is grave and so is the answer. If, for any long period, wages rise faster than productivity, then the alternatives are either unemployment and diminished production or continuous inflation. It is, of course, possible to conceive that some small increases of wages can be financed out of profits without serious reactions on employment. But the statistical limits are small, and it is to treat the subject with less seriousness than it deserves to assume that there is any long-lasting solution in this direction. Exactly the same problem would exist were all industry nationalized and all profits appropriated by the state: if wage-rates rose faster than productivity, the main alternatives would be unemployment or inflation.

But are we right in assuming that such a development is inevitable? I see no ground for a pessimism as deep as this. As I have argued above, I do not believe that the greater part of the inflation which has taken place already is to be explained in these terms. On my conception, up to recently the rise of wages has usually been the *result*, not the *cause*, of the general inflation. When the demand for labour in most parts of the economy so much exceeded the supply, the trade union leaders would have had to be angels not to cash in on the situation. If they had not been there, it is improbable that the rise would have been much less.

But now the situation has changed. For the time being, at least, the demand inflation is at an end. The funds out of which it was financed are under more control — at least, let us hope they are. And the question what in the new conditions will be the policy of the leaders of the unions is not yet solved. I am not one of those who believe that much good is to be expected from mere exhortation to any section of the community; if I had been a trade union leader during the last few years I should have become positively neurotic at the barrage of appeals to my patriotism, social solidarity, sense of decency, and so on and so forth. But it is not at all obvious to me that trade union leaders are so indifferent to their own interest as to persist long in policies liable to create unemployment, if inflationary finance is not there. This is not to say that I should expect the ending of a period of inflation to be free of friction or that I believe that people in such positions are incapable of mistaking for a time where their true interests lie — the trade unions of this country for years have clung to restrictive practices which in the long run help no one. But it would surely be very short-sighted policy for any government to assume that such responsible bodies are incapable of learning from experience and to base policy upon the assumption that they will always react one way whatever the general state of the economy.

Whether this be true or not, my conception of the duty of governments in this connection is clear. It is not the duty of governments to make the maintenance of employment the be-all and end-all of policy, regardless of what happens to the value of money. It is their duty rather to maintain conditions which will make a high level of employment compatible with a stable value of money. They should not say we guarantee employment whatever demands are made in respect of wage-rates; they should say rather we will try to maintain such a volume of expenditure as, given an income-level rising with productivity, will maintain a high level of employment. If they do this, then, in a free society at any rate, it is for trade unionists and all the rest of us to decide how we react as regards the prices we put on our own particular products.

This, clearly, is a controversial view. There are many who hold that salvation lies in a much more authoritarian direction. Control of wages from the centre, plus some measure of dividend limitation, is the solution they favour. My solution is in quite conscious opposition to this. I do not think that experience elsewhere suggests that in the absence of deliberate monetary stabilization, a general wage control is likely to be successful; and, if monetary stabilization is attempted, such a control seems to me unnecessary. I have no desire at this time of day to see the whole apparatus of independent trade unionism, which has performed such valuable services in the past, sacrificed in so dubious an enterprise. I think it is more compatible with the principles of a free society that we should be free to make mistakes and to learn from them than that we should be clamped down by a system of regulation from the centre which, if experience elsewhere is anything to go by, is itself no less liable to error.

To return, however, to the theory of continuing inflation, perhaps the ultimate criticism here is that the thing is extremely unlikely to work out as planned. I should be willing to concede that, *if* there could take place an inflation of, say, $\frac{1}{2}$ or even 1 per cent per annum, and that *if* this could go on unperceived and unanticipated, then there might be important advantages. There would be a mild reinforcement of the power to accumulate in the shape of higher money earnings on the part of companies and employers. There would be elbow room for the process of collective bargaining to make small mistakes of rate-fixing without causing unemployment. Against this, there would be some injustice to the owners of fixed interest-bearing securities and the recipients of incomes which are only adjusted at long intervals. But experience of periods of mild gold inflation tends to suggest that on balance there would be substantial prosperity.

But all this depends upon the assumption that the process is unanticipated and, until it has happened, unperceived. If, after a time, people become alive to what is happening, still more if they come to assume that a certain decline in the value of money is one of the necessary concomitants of accepted policy, then they will adjust their plans accordingly and none of the beneficial by-products of their failing to see what was going on will be present. Lenders will not lend, save for a higher rate of interest. Contracts will not be concluded, save with a margin allowing for the expected rate of depreciation.[1] What is more, after a time, the difficulties tend to be cumulative. The fear of inflation tends to create more inflation. Most of the hyper-inflations of history were gradual to begin with, but they ended in something not at all gradual.

All this would apply to a community without external economic relations or where the external factor was relatively unimportant. Where, however, external relations loom large in the economic structure, as they do in ours, the effects of inflation are apt to be much more immediate and much more serious. If the inflation is not only absolute but relative, if, that is to say, it is greater than any such movement which is going on elsewhere, then the effects on the balance of payments show themselves very quickly. It is not a matter of danger in the long period, it is a matter of danger in a very few months. And this, of course, is particularly germane to our situation. I can imagine a mild inflation in the United States proceeding without overmuch difficulty for several, perhaps for many, years. I cannot conceive such a development in this country. If we go on inflating, and if our inflation is greater than is going on in important countries elsewhere, then — as indeed we know from the recurrent crises of the post-war period — the effect is likely to be sharp and sudden. And I do not think

[1] If in addition to this, some of the recent apologists for inflation had their way and all pensions and fixed interest obligations of the government were put on a sliding scale basis so that absolutely no one suffered, then, of course, all incentive would have gone out of the process and we should be exactly where we were before.

that our peculiar system, with its world-wide ramifications depending essentially on a particular kind of understanding and confidence, can stand an indefinite succession of crises.

But that brings me to the last point which I wish to make in this already overlong paper. For the next few years at least, an objective, second only in importance to the avoidance of inflation or deflation, must be the strengthening of the reserve. With our capital account in its present condition, our reserves are quite inadequate. We are trying to be bankers for a large part of the world, but we are not prepared to keep a reserve large enough to preclude crises of confidence. In such conditions, rumours which, were the reserves at all adequate, would exhaust themselves in light gossip, tend to start major convulsions. The position is not permanently viable, and it should be a major objective of policy to put it right.

It is sometimes said that this is impossible. We have done all we can since the war and yet there is no improvement. The only way in which the reserve position can be improved is by some gigantic international operation. Failing this, we should set our sights at a lower target and resign ourselves to the mediocrity of our position.

This argument seems to me to lack substance. I am no foe to international action in regard to this problem, and I would greet with enthusiasm action of the kind suggested by Sir Oliver Franks in his recent annual statement.[1] But I do not agree that, if international action is slow in developing, there is nothing that we can do to help ourselves. I cannot see any justification for this, either in theory or experience. Other countries have increased their reserves. Why should not we? What is so different in the condition of Germany and ourselves that while, on balance, our reserve has not increased at all since the summer of 1950, in the same period the German reserve has mounted from $260 millions to some $4000 millions? Doubtless there are many inessential differences which can be cited one way or the other. But the main

---

[1] See the *Economist*, January 25th, 1958, pp. 350–3.

difference, I submit, is that the Germans have had the will to do this thing and we have not. And let no one say that this has been accomplished at the price of poverty and stagnation. Between 1950 and 1957, while our real output per head has increased by about 15 per cent, the German has risen by nearly 60 per cent.

Is it not the bankruptcy of statesmanship and national morale to argue that this sort of thing is impossible for us?

# 10

## MONETARY THEORY AND
## THE RADCLIFFE REPORT [1]

### I

THE Report of the Radcliffe Committee is a document which covers a great variety of topics relating to the working of the British monetary system. The present structure of the London Capital Market, the external position of sterling, the relations between the Bank of England and the government, a wealth of highly significant financial statistics hitherto inaccessible — if it were only for its contribution in respect of any of these, it would still take its place as one of the most important publications of its kind in the long course of British monetary history.

Nevertheless, if we are considering the progress of economic thought in general and of monetary theory in particular, I would venture the conjecture that it is for its pronouncements in this respect that it will be chiefly considered by the future historian. Whether we agree with it or disagree with it, it has set us all thinking again upon the ultimate problems, and it is safe to say that, whichever way the controversies which it has aroused are ultimately decided, things will never be quite the same again. It is with this aspect of the Report, therefore, that I have chosen to deal in this paper.

Broadly speaking, the main theoretical interest of the Report arises in two connections: its analysis of the nature of the monetary mechanism and its verdict on the effectiveness of its use. In what I have to say, therefore, I shall

[1] A paper read before Professor Papi's seminar at the University of Rome in the spring of 1960. In preparing it for final publication I have amplified it a little in places and included some comment on Professor Sayers' important presidential address at the meeting of the British Association in the autumn of that year.

follow the same order. I shall discuss mechanisms first and effectiveness second. Then in a final section I shall make certain observations about consequences for policy.

That is all I need say about the justification and plan of this paper. But since in general my approach and my conclusions will be somewhat critical, I should like to make it clear from the outset that my differences with the Committee are wholly intellectual. Four of the signatories of the Report are very good friends of mine and all are men for whose integrity and intellectual power I have the greatest possible respect. So that, although in the interest of clarity I shall put my points as forcibly as I can, I differ from the Committee with regret and with full recognition that it may be I, and not they, who will eventually be proved to be wrong. But the points at issue are pretty fundamental and, at this stage, I think our common interest in the advancement of knowledge is best served by setting forth with friendly candour the grounds of difference.

II

Let me begin then with the theory of the mechanism.

Economic theory at the present day is not in so advanced a state that it is possible to point to any one account of the nature of the monetary machine which, before the publication of this report, might be said to have commanded general acceptance. The discussions of specific practical problems, which were the moulds of so much rule-of-thumb lore in this respect, naturally involved different emphasis in different cases. And the models with which pure theory devised its first approximations, were recognized to involve such simplification as to leave out features which might be of great importance in practical life. Moreover, it would have been generally acknowledged that, in most monetary centres, there was enough of market imperfection and conventional behaviour as to warrant some degree of eclecticism in dealing with particular situations as, for instance, the habit of the Federal Reserve Board in operating both with variations of reserve requirements and variations of rates of discount.

Nevertheless, it is probably not claiming too much to say that there would have been a very considerable measure of support for the view that the central feature of the picture, or at least the central instrument of control, was the supply of money in the sense of cash and appropriately defined bank deposits. This implied no denial of the importance of interest rates or qualitative control of credit which, on this view, were all linked very closely with this ultimate control: the emphasis on supply is simply an emphasis on something immediately subject to control and something which can be conceived in some way or other to govern other connected instruments. As Mr. Riefler of the Federal Reserve Board said in the course of evidence which well represented this mode of approach, 'The fundamental thing we do is to operate on the reserve position. If we ever forget that, we are gone' (Evidence, Q.9818).[1]

The Radcliffe Committee definitely challenge this conception. As I shall indicate later, it is perhaps not altogether certain how far this challenge goes. But its existence is clear. After describing the view I have just outlined (para. 388), they go on to say, 'Our view is different. Though we do not regard the supply of money as an unimportant quantity, we view it as only part of the wider structure of liquidity in the economy' (para. 389). And later, 'We therefore follow Professor Kahn in insisting on the structure of interest rates rather than some notion of the supply of money as the centrepiece of monetary action' (para. 395); and again, 'We find control of the supply of money to be no more than an important facet of debt management' (para. 514).

After some months of discussion, it is still not easy to say exactly what all this means in relation to the doctrine

---

[1] The inset references are to the *Report of the Committee on the Working of the Monetary System*, Cmd. 827, 1959, or to the Minutes of Evidence. References to the latter give the question number, references to the Report itself merely give the paragraph.

challenged, though perhaps Professor Sayers' half playful suggestion that the quantity theorist of the future might find 'clearing bank deposits to be the small change of the monetary system' has done something to sharpen the contrast and to indicate historical analogies.[1]  But before proceeding to analysis of the differences, there is an important preliminary to be disposed of — an explanation of the effects of *bank* liquidity on the supply of money in the British system. For until this has been provided there is some danger of controversy at cross purposes.

### (a)  *Treasury Bills and the Supply of Money*

Up to a very recent date, the common account of the working of the British monetary system would certainly attribute the control of the supply of money to the Bank of England *via* its control of the so-called credit base.  The deposit-creating power of the banks was said to be limited by the necessity of observing a conventional ratio between the total deposits and the reserves of cash and deposits at the Bank of England, and these reserves were said to be capable of easy regulation by the policy of the Bank of England.  If the position was considered to be too easy, then it would be dealt with by the sale of securities, which would be paid for in ways which would necessarily reduce bankers' deposits at the Bank of England : if it was too tight, then the purchase of securities by the bank would increase them.

This account may have been reasonably adequate before 1914, but it had certainly ceased to be true when it was given its classic form in the report of the Macmillan Committee. And it is completely out of relation to the realities of the present day.

The reason for this is to be found in the existence of a great volume of short-term government debt in the form of Treasury bills and the preponderance of such instruments in the banks' portfolios of liquid reserves.  This brings it about that if the banks find their 'cash' reserves depleted by the open market policy of the Bank of England, then they can

[1] *Economic Journal*, vol. lxx, p. 724.

virtually force a reversal of this position by allowing Treasury bills to run off. For unless the government is willing to reduce its borrowing or to raise its funds by long-term issues to the public, the net effect of the running off of Treasury bills which have been in the hands of the banks, is that the government raises the money it needs by borrowing from the Bank of England and this recreates the reserves of the joint stock banks which had originally been destroyed. The uncovering of the technical details involved in this process is one of the most important achievements of monetary analysis of the last few years. Like many such discoveries, it seems to have dawned on several people more or less at the same time; conspicuously Mr. Dacey and Professor Sayers.[1]

The implications for policy are very considerable. It means in effect that control of credit has passed from the Bank of England to the Treasury. Doubtless, in the very short run, the Bank of England can influence the technical position with the instruments still at its disposal. But, in general, if the trend of money supply is to be controlled it must be through control of the Treasury bill issue — or by special regulations bearing directly upon the volume of bank deposits. And this is no mere speculative diagnosis. Mr. Dacey has published a series of remarkable graphs showing the extent to which the liquid assets of the clearing banks and the market supply of Treasury bills tend to move in harmony.[2]

Now the relevance of all this to the main theme of this paper is as follows. If the Radcliffe Committee had said that the supply of liquidity, in the shape of market Treasury bills, governed the supply of money and that for this reason, this, rather than the supply of money, was to be considered as the focal point of policy, then so far as I am concerned, there would have been very little ground for cavil — indeed only enthusiastic agreement. But although, as Mr. Dacey has shown, such a position can very easily be based on the

---

[1] See references above p. 175 n. There is some reason to suppose that the Bank of England had been conscious of the change in its powers for a very considerable time. [2] *Money under Review*, chapter v, *passim*.

material which they furnish, this is not the position of the Committee or their challenge to the position of the supply of money in the general theory of monetary policy up to now. Bank liquidity in this narrow sense as one of the main factors governing the supply of money in the wide sense is not the so-called liquidity of the system as a whole which the Radcliffe Committee put in the centre of their picture.

To this conception therefore we must now turn.

(b) *Interest Rates* versus *Supply of Money*

Let us begin by trying to state in very broad terms the central features of the Committee's position.

The problem which confronts them at this stage in the argument is to show what part of the monetary mechanism is to be regarded as having the leading significance as a potential instrument of control.

In approaching this problem they start from the level of aggregate demand. The immediate influence on economic activity — on prices and employment — is obviously the volume of spending, and this, as we know, can be regarded as deriving from two main streams: investment (in the Keynesian sense), and consumption.

But investment in turn depends on two influences: the incentive to invest and what the Committee call the liquidity position of the community. And both of these are themselves dependent upon interest rates. It follows, therefore, that the structure of interest rates is to be regarded as the main instrument of policy — as the Committee put it, 'as the centre piece of monetary action'. The rôle of the supply of money is simply to set rates of interest.

Now at first sight it might be thought that all this is simply a slightly different way of stating the theory which I have suggested to be prevalent prior to the labours of the Committee.

Thus, all of us would accept the rate of spending or aggregate demand as the influence through which monetary policy seeks to operate. (The final objective of such policy — high employment, stable prices, external equilibrium, economic growth, and so on — are clearly matters of ends rather than means in this context and need not complicate the argument at this juncture.)

All, too, would agree that 'the state of liquidity' — in some sense or other — was an influence on spending; although, as we shall see later, there is considerable room for doubting whether, in this connection, the Committee have altogether succeeded in adequately formulating their conception. No exposition of monetary theory known to me denies the influence on spending of the demand for money, even though this may sometimes be described in terms of the velocity of circulation. And the demand for money is very obviously, in part, a function of the extent of non-monetary liquidity.[1] That is to say, the extent to which it is possible to achieve a certain effect on the rate of spending by manipulating the supply of money, will therefore vary with the extent to which near-money substitutes are available.

Furthermore, we should all agree that the incentive to invest and the liquidity of the community as a whole are affected by the structure of interest rates. Indeed, as will be seen later, some of us are disposed to attach considerably more influence to these instruments than the Committee.

And, finally, we should all agree that the structure of interest rates was affected by the supply of money.

So that, at first sight, it might seem to be simply a matter of alternative emphasis; and it might well be that appropriateness of one way of putting things rather than the other depends upon the particular problem which is under discussion. We all agree that, in matters of this sort, the influences at work are multiple. It is only in regard to questions of *control* that any single factor can be regarded as ultimate; and even here there is legitimate scope for a considerable degree of eclecticism.

It is quite clear, however, from the passages which I have quoted, that the Committee do not take this view. Rightly or wrongly, they are convinced that they are inviting us to

[1] On this, see a very forceful analysis by Professor Paish entitled "What is this Liquidity", in his *Studies in an Inflationary Economy*, pp. 70–9.

step into a completely new pair of trousers — to use Keynes' famous phrase ; and throughout their exposition they speak as if any explanation which starts from the supply of money is not merely a legitimate way of approach alternative to their own but rather one which is definitely misleading and even erroneous. Professor Sayers' citation of what he suggests to be parallel differences in the historic controversies between the Banking School and the Currency School bears out this interpretation. There was certainly a head-on collision there.

At first, when I read the Report, I thought this emphasis exaggerated — and said so in a public notice. But I have gradually come to think that it is correct and that cumulatively, what may, at first sight, appear to be minor divergences do in fact add up to major differences, not merely in analysis but still more in historical interpretation and recommendations for policy. But this is something which can only be shown in the course of detailed discussion.


### III

Let me therefore address myself to setting forth the points at which I take issue with the Committee's analysis and the reasons why I regard the approach *via* the supply of money to be preferable. They fall into four groups.

(*a*) My first criticism relates to the conception of liquidity and the rôle it plays in the Committee's general outlook. There seem to be ambiguities here which go far to elide very fundamental distinctions.

Thus, when we speak of the liquidity of an individual conceived to be acting alone, it is clear that our conception includes both his money in the sense of currency and bank deposits, and his assets, such as bills and securities which he can dispose in various markets without appreciable loss. There are differences of risk involved which are well known and important to the prudent conduct of business ; but, in the first approximation at any rate, the idea is workable and unlikely to mislead.

But when we come to speak of the liquidity of the community as a whole, the conception which plays so large a part in the thought of the Committee, modifications are necessary and it becomes very important to distinguish between the liquidity which consists of money and the liquidity which does not. *For non-monetary liquidity* — the extent to which the assets involved can be realized without any great upset of values — *depends upon the availability of liquidity in a monetary form.* This is a distinction which has very important analytical implications. Yet there is a passage in paragraph 395 where the Committee seem to go out of their way to repudiate it, saying that 'the behaviour of bank deposits is only of interest because it has some bearing . . . on the behaviour of other lenders'. Sir Dennis Robertson, who draws attention to this passage, adds the mordant comment, 'Yes, indeed it has [some bearing] since it is bank deposits *alias* money, that these other lenders lend'.[1]

Needless to say, to emphasize this distinction and its analytical significance is not in the least to deny the importance of non-monetary liquidity. It would be universally acknowledged that the extent of non-monetary liquidity is a very significant factor affecting the demand for monetary liquidity. Other things being equal, the demand for money at any price level and any structure of interest rates must be less in a community well supplied with easily marketable stock exchange securities than it would be in a community in which all assets other than money consisted in highly specific stocks or instruments of production. All that is contended here is that the distinction is real and important and that any analysis which elides it is likely to overlook relationships of pivotal significance. In particular — and this is especially germane to the theme I am developing — it is likely to overlook the extent to which the non-monetary liquidity of the system as a whole is a function of the elasticity of supply of money.

(*b*) My second criticism is even more fundamental.

1 *The Banker,* December 1959, p. 720.

While, as I have suggested above, it ought not to be impossible to reconcile theories of the monetary mechanism which work *backwards* from the flow of expenditure — as does the Committee — with theories which work *forwards* from the supply of money — as do various versions of the Quantity Theory — I see no such possibility here. For, unless I misunderstand them grossly, the Committee's conception of the analytical status of the money supply is something which is quite irreconcilable with any form of the Quantity Theory.

This conception emerges most sharply in the much quoted paragraph 391 in which the Committee give their reasons for rejecting any analysis involving the idea of velocity of circulation. '*We cannot find*', they say, '*any reason for supposing, or any experience in monetary history indicating any limit to the velocity of circulation*' [my italics]. It is difficult to imagine a more clear-cut statement or more emphatic words. But, if it is true, then obviously the supply of money is a matter of very little significance. Any change in its magnitude can be compensated by an inverse change in the velocity of circulation, *i.e.* in the demand for money. Any hope that it can be controlled in such a way as to exercise a stabilizing influence is, therefore, groundless. Indeed, it is difficult to see even how, save in the very shortest of short periods, it can have much influence in setting rates of interest — a function which, oddly enough, the Committee seems disposed to allow.

But is it true? It is certainly true that there is no unalterable demand function for money, regardless of time and place — any more than there are fixed demand functions of this sort for any other commodity or convenience. It is true, further, that the demand for money has in fact shifted through time with the discovery and elaboration of other means of making payments and that — a circumstance which seems greatly to have impressed the Committee — a high price for money, in the shape of high interest rates, may provide a positive inducement to such developments. It is true, finally, that the demand for money may well change with changing expectations: this is exemplified, both in the flight from money which develops during the latter stages of hyper-inflation and in the considerable extension of trade credit which takes place during the early stages of a boom.

All this, it is to be hoped, is common property. But the question remains whether, at any particular time, there are no limits to the diminution of the demand for money, that is to say, to the increase of the velocity of circulation; so that any diminution in supply will automatically *and indefinitely* be offset by changes on the demand side. That seems to me, in contradistinction to the signatories of the Report, to have little support in either reason or experience. But that is the question which is raised by their downright assertion.

Consider first the pure theory of the subject. The size of the holdings which individuals will try to maintain, given the price level and the structure of interest rates, is not an arbitrary matter. It is to be assumed to be determined by rough estimates of the comparative amenity, at the margin, of holding units of wealth in that form rather than in some other; and just as we may assume that, if the stock were increased, the marginal amenity gained would be less than could be gained by holding an equivalent amount in some other form, so we must assume that, if it were diminished, the marginal amenity lost would be greater than could be gained elsewhere. This suggests that, as the supply of money available to the community as a whole diminishes, if other things remain the same, there is likely to be a fall in aggregate expenditure. The inconvenience of the smaller stocks must lead some individuals at least to seek to rehabilitate their position. Now it may well be that here, as in the case of other goods and services, the changes consequent on the initial diminution of supply may induce a search for new substitutes. There is no reason whatever to deny this possibility; and if this were to happen and to be successful the result could be described as a diminution of demand for money or an increase of the velocity of circulation. But it would certainly be most improbable that then and there, or indeed within a measurable period of time, such changes could proceed *without limit*, so that, whatever the diminution of supply, no inconvenience need be caused and no efforts to reconstitute cash holdings. The idea that an induced search for money substitutes can bring it about that the short-term demand curve for money has an infinite elasticity backwards seems to me to lack plausibility.

This conclusion surely harmonizes with experience. The occasions where velocity has appeared to have no limits have been the great hyper-inflations where expectation of further depreciation (due, be it here noted, to the absence of limits on money supply) has led people to wish to disembarrass themselves altogether of the money in question and to substitute other moneys or other goods. In normal circumstances, there seems no evidence of the likelihood of velocity varying without limits. We know, as I have pointed out already, that there is a certain variation within cyclical movements. But what statistical evidence there is, is all against the absence of limits. Recent investigations of this subject by Professor Friedman and his associates seem to suggest a quite remarkable constancy over medium periods, if related to average income rather than to momentary changes.[1]

Furthermore, the evidence that over time the supply of money has a positive influence one way or the other is really very considerable. The suggestion, implied by Professor Sayers' references to deposits as small change and to the Banking School, that the money supply is to be regarded as something passive which adapts itself to movements of income and expenditure leaves much to be explained in the broad perspective of history, which, on the alternative view, is easily comprehensible. If we look at the influence of the great gold and silver discoveries it is really very difficult to deny some causal influence on movements of prices and trade: any suggestion — which I do not believe for a moment that Professor Sayers would countenance — that the introduction into circulation of money made of these metals was in some sense of secondary significance, would

---

[1] See *Studies in the Quantity Theory of Money* (Chicago, 1956), particularly section I.

be highly unplausible.  Nor does the history of paper inflations suggest any less positive an influence — think, for instance, of the episode of the Assignats.  Similarly, if we look at the history of deflations, although it would be wrong to suggest that the supply factor was the only monetary influence, it would not be wrong to say that there are very few instances of things going conspicuously wrong in this respect where there has not been some reduction of money supply or at least failure of supply to keep pace with obvious needs.

My own view of these matters could not be more vividly expressed than it was nearly two hundred years ago by Arthur Young in his *Political Arithmetic*.  Sir James Steuart, whose greatly neglected *Political Economy* may be regarded as a sort of compendium of all subsequent anti-quantitative theories of money, had expressed views which in broad outline anticipate in a striking way the sentiments of the Radcliffe Committee.  'Let the specie of a country', he says, 'be augmented or diminished in ever so great a proportion, commodities will still rise and fall according to the principles of demand and competition, and these will constantly depend upon the inclinations of those who have *property* or any kind of *equivalent* whatsoever to give, but never upon the quantity of coin they are possessed of.' [1]

On which Young comments, 'Sir James will keep close to the circumstance that the quantity of money has nothing to do in the case, if a man will not *spend* when he possesses : but this appears to me to be taken for granted ; relative to a market day, or other point of competition I admit of it : but I think it should be rejected on application to a period. . . . I have no idea of a great increase of national wealth (meaning here, money) without an increase of the expenses of individuals following.' [2]

This seems to me to hit the nail on the head completely.  The Radcliffe Committee are certainly dead right in insisting that the immediate determinant of the price level and the general level of activity is the volume of expenditure which

[1] Steuart, *op. cit.* vol. i, pp. 400-1.    [2] Young, *op. cit.* pp. 114-15.

derives, not only from the money supply but also from trade credit and all sorts of money substitutes : and if any reputable quantity theorist since Hume has denied this, let him be forever disgraced. But in making this the pretext for relegating the supply of money to a subordinate, and even passive position, the Committee, like the Banking School and many others before them, seem to me to be in danger of an error of analytical perspective no less one-sided in pure theory and even more damaging in practice than that of those — if they exist — who ignore the short period vicissitudes of velocity and trade credit.

(c) But this brings me to my third criticism. The perspective of the Committee appears to me to be awry not only in its denials but also in its affirmations. Not only do they seem to underestimate and misconceive the rôle of the supply of money but, further, the substitute which they propose as 'the centre piece of monetary policy', the structure of interest rates, appears to be in the wrong place and to occupy a disproportionate position in the picture.

Now if there were only one rate of interest, as in Wicksell's famous model, and if all variations in expenditure were financed by borrowing in a unified capital market, it might well be held to be a matter of indifference which to emphasize first, the rate of interest or the supply of money. A monopolist producer of some unique mineral water can be conceived to proceed either by fixing his price or by regulating supply — if he is aiming to maximize profits, the result should be the same in the end — the price fixed should result in the volume of sales which achieves this object equally with fixing of sales at a point which secures the optimal price.

But, of course, the real world has not this degree of simplicity. The various branches of the capital market, although interconnected, as the Committee admirably insist, are not completely unified. There is not one, there are many rates of interest. And the interrelations between markets and rates are such that if, either in thought or in action, you start only with one, you are liable to encounter all sorts of difficulties. It is extraordinarily difficult to say how one rate works, unless, at the same time, you say a great deal about all the others. This is not to be taken as an argument for never operating *via* one rate or relying on one rate to lead. But it is a reminder that any attempt to fix rates and their relationship is a much more complex proceeding than one which begins from variations of money supply, leaving the consequential variations of rates to be determined at least in part by the markets.

Furthermore, it is not realistic to speak as if all variations of expenditure involving variations of money supply occur *via* the influence of interest rates. Credit rationing which we know to play a large part in determining the volume of expenditure may operate without changes in interest rates; and government spending involving inflationary borrowing from the central bank and hence increases of money supply, depends very little on the interest rate fixed for such transactions. This has been surely quite as important in the causation of the historic inflations as Wicksellian interest rates fixed below the level which would equate borrowing and lending if savings took place *in natura*.

I venture to submit that explanations of the monetary mechanism which begin from the supply of money and the influences which may cause it to vary, are less liable to overlook such factors than explanations which regard the structure of interest rates as 'the centrepiece of monetary policy'.

(*d*) Finally, there is the question of control. My chief reason for putting the supply of money in the foreground of the picture is not in the least that I want to ignore or to dwarf the importance of other elements in the mechanism or even other instruments of control, but rather because it is so much the most obvious and easily available instrument. I have no objection in principle to control *via* the Bank Rate or any other rate which is amenable. In any likely crisis I am sure I should want to use many instruments at once. But it is surely obvious that it is the supply of money which is most generally susceptible to control. To attempt directly to control the whole range of interest rates is a very formid-able task. Indeed, it is not at all certain how far it can be done directly at the long end without causing more trouble than good. Whereas control of the credit base is in concep-tion and in principle relatively straightforward. As we have seen, in the present conditions of the British money market, this may not be so for the Bank of England if the volume of Treasury bills outstanding is excessive. But if for this reason the Bank is relatively impotent, this cannot be said of the government; and if the government is willing to work with the Bank in this respect rather than against it, there is no reason why the control of money supply should be regarded as impracticable.

But this brings me to the second main division of this enquiry, the effects of the use of this mechanism.

IV

The Committee do not take a very sanguine view of the possibilities of monetary policy.

As we have seen, the instruments of their choice — interest rates — are supposed to operate through two influ-ences on aggregate demand — the incentive to invest and the general liquidity of the community.

So far as the first of these is concerned, effects *via* the incentive to invest, the Committee take a very poor view indeed. According to their findings, interest rates have no influence to speak of on the holding of stocks, either of primary products or manufactures. They admit some effects on long-term investment. But these are thought to be slow and perhaps not very extensive. Moreover, in recent years they have been blunted by taxation and important sectors have been removed from their sphere of influence.

Hence, if the situation is to be saved at all it must be chiefly *via* the so-called liquidity effect. If rates of interest rise, there is an immediate effect on the liquidity position of potential lenders. The Committee argue that, in theory at any rate, here, at least, movements of interest rates can act more rapidly, though since movements of the long-term rate are involved, it is just as well not to be too hopeful.

Armed with this analysis, the Committee make some examination of the monetary history of the fifties. They admit that interest rates might with advantage have been higher during the early years. But, despite the episode of 1957–58, they go on to urge that it is difficult to find any very outstanding evidence of the positive influence of monetary policy. They express the hope that perhaps during the sixties conditions may be more favourable. But in general I do not think it is unfair to say that one gains the impression of quiet resignation to the relative unimportance of such policies — so much so, indeed, that theorists of the extreme left have hailed the Report as a justification for pressing for more direct controls. As I have said elsewhere, they believe in monetary policy but they do not believe in it very much.

I do not find it necessary to adopt so pessimistic an attitude. Provided that governments are prepared to use it with reasonable determination, I do not see why we need regard monetary policy as having such limited potentialities.

Before I explain the reasons for this, I should like, however, to make it as plain as I can that I am not arguing for sole reliance upon monetary policy. I find it desirable to emphasize this point, since, despite most explicit words to that effect in my written evidence, I was cross-examined in a friendly way by a member of the Committee as though I had said exactly the contrary. Let me, therefore, say in italicized words that, in my opinion, *in the strongly inflationary conditions of the post-war period, I am clear that sole reliance on monetary policy would have been both unwise and undesirable.* I am equally clear that this would have been so had we run into a deflationary situation. I suppose it is naïve to hope to be judged by what one says rather than by some accidental mythology. But there, for what it is worth, is my conviction on this subject, held firmly since before the end of the war and expressed in several publications.

But having said this, may I come back to my main theme

by saying that in my judgment the Committee radically underestimate the contribution which can be made by monetary policy. I hold this opinion, both on grounds of theory and of experience; and the remainder of this part of my remarks will be devoted to setting these forth.

Let me begin with the theory of the subject and in this connection deal first with the incentive to invest.

Let me say at once that I fully accept that part of the Committee's analysis which deals with the blunting effect on this incentive of high direct taxation and with the limitation of its potential scope by the quasi-insulation of nationalized industry. I agree that *if*, with taxation at its present level, central banks are still to regard themselves as limited to a range of manipulations of the structure of interest rates which would only be fully effective if it were at a lower level and *if* governments are to conduct their own business without regard to the relative scarcity of funds for investment, then certainly the effectiveness of any measures working through interest rates and the supply of money will be limited.

Nevertheless, I venture to suggest that the Committee considerably underestimate the potential effects of such policies. After all, an admission of the limitations just discussed is no criticism of monetary policy as such: it is only a criticism of the schizoid tendencies of governments who are not prepared to co-ordinate means and ends. My criticism of the Committee in this connection is, not that they acknowledge these adventitious impediments but rather that their exposition of the theory of the subject tends to underestimate the potentialities of monetary policy in general. This for three main reasons.

First, as I have indicated already, their concentration on the effects of interest rates as such leaves out all sorts of things which may happen even if rates do not move. The many possibilities of credit rationing which we know in fact to be imposed, if the credit base is reduced, tend to fall out of view. Yet even if some business witnesses beat their breasts and declare their total insensibility to changes in interest rates, we know that they are certainly not indifferent to the availability of credit.

Secondly, I think that the Committee dismisses in much too cavalier a fashion the possible effects on the demand for stocks of changes in interest rates. It is, of course, quite obvious that this can be overshadowed by other factors. Yet general considerations of the narrowness of profit margins on turnover in such businesses certainly suggest that it is improbable that the effects, in stimulating or retarding orders, of changing interest charges are negligible. This is admittedly a highly controversial subject and attempts to test the theory by reference to fact have not so far been very successful. But I am not impressed by the Committee's handling of the subject, and I suspect that Sir Ralph Hawtrey has established a case to be considered when he argues that some at least of the evidence tends against their conclusion.[1]

Thirdly, when we come to consider investment plans in general it is probably true that it takes some time for the *nature* of such plans to be extensively affected by changes in interest rates. But this does not mean that their *volume* may not be considerably affected within a very much shorter period, especially if the changes are not expected to be long lasting. The effects on aggregate demand of the postponement or acceleration of putting plans into operation seems to me to be potentially greater than the Committee seem to recognize.

Let me now turn to the so-called liquidity effect, still keeping for the time being on the plane of pure theory.

As I have pointed out already, it is on this effect that the Committee chiefly relies for any faith that it may retain in the efficiency of monetary policy. Nevertheless, even here, they seem to me to show a considerable tendency to underestimate its potential scope and power.

Why is this? I am inclined to think that part at least of the answer is to be found in their persistent emphasis in this context on changes in the disposition of *lenders*. I suggest

[1] See *The Banker's Magazine*, May 1960, pp. 410-18.

that this is much too narrow: indeed, I doubt whether it is the centre of the picture. For changes in capital values due to changes in interest rates affect not only lenders but *spenders* generally — both companies spending on development out of their own resources and individuals spending out of capital or income. In either case a fall in capital values due to an upward change in interest rates leads to a disposition to hold back and to reconstitute losses by saving. And, even if saving does not take place, the impulse to hold back is still operative — especially if, as might easily be the case in certain phases of the trade cycle, the losses are expected to be transitory. This effect seems to me to be extremely important. If, to get clear of the ambiguities and limitations of the concept of liquidity, it were rechristened the *wealth* effect, it would surely be recognized as an influence operating on a very wide front indeed. We all know that rates of expenditure should be regarded as being dependent not only on rates of income but also upon the magnitude of capital, in whatever form it happens to be held.

So much for the theory of the subject. When we turn to practical testing we are on even more debatable ground. So many things happen at once that the isolation of causal factors must necessarily be a matter of intense intellectual difficulty. Nevertheless, it seems to me that, much as there is still to be done in this field, the general weight of evidence tends to sustain the view that monetary policy is potentially effective and to refute the view that it is not.

Let me draw attention first to a very characteristic feature of the general debate about policy which, in my judgment, at least, constitutes a pretty strong presumption that some very positive influence is involved. I refer to the widespread complaints of the effects of dear money and credit restriction. I see no reason whatever to dismiss these as without foundation. It is all very well for the Committee to point to the assertions of some prominent business men that changes in interest rates have no influence on their operations. If this is so, we are surely entitled to ask why the almost universal howl whenever policies of this sort are put into serious operation? Are we to suppose that it is entirely due to disinterested apprehension regarding the burden of the national debt and interest payments to overseas creditors? Speaking as one who has listened very intently to this sort of thing on many occasions, I must say that it does not sound that way. And I personally would assert roundly that I just do not believe that, for the majority of business men, the fear of dear money and credit restriction can coexist with complete indifference in practice to what actually happens.

When we turn to the actual course of history, I find it very difficult to believe that the evidence tells *against* the view that monetary policy is a valuable instrument for controlling inflation, though I am inclined to believe that it would be less favourable to the hope that deflation is always susceptible to the same treatment. On the contrary, I would have thought that, in the main, the record tells quite definitely the other way. Certainly, my general impression is that after both World Wars I and II, whenever monetary policy has been vigorously used (if necessary, in combination with other policies), it has shown itself capable of playing an essential part in curbing inflation. Think, for instance, of the Belgian surgical operation or the German currency reform. Similarly, with the history of more moderate episodes. The financial history of Europe since the war seems to show that where monetary policy has been tried with reasonable persistence and appropriateness, it succeeds. At any rate, I should say that the onus rests on those who argue differently, to demonstrate that in each case, the apparent success was due to the happy coincidence of some other influence.

But what about our own experience in the United Kingdom? The Committee do not definitely say that the episode of 1957 is not evidence in favour of the effectiveness of monetary policy — although, of course, we have had elsewhere the usual crop of explanations in terms of the fortunate arrival of gods in the machine in the shape of falling raw material price, spontaneous internal readjustments, and so on and so forth. But considering that it happened before their eyes when they were sitting, they maintain a most curious reserve about it all. Personally, although recognizing the complexity of the situation and the considerable influence of other measures, I do not think that the stabilization of the situation can be completely interpreted without giving considerable influence to the pretty strong monetary measures which were actually adopted.

The scepticism of the Committee — or, shall I say, their agnosticism? — is, however, chiefly displayed in regard to the earlier period. As I have said already, they are inclined to urge that interest rates were probably too low. But instead of regarding this circumstance as evidence in favour of the view that in the absence of appropriate monetary policy things are likely to go seriously wrong, they spend much time expatiating on the weakness of the effect of what monetary restraints were actually adopted. It is in this connection that they seem to have been so adversely impressed by the testimony of some of their business witnesses.

On all this it is possible to agree with the statement of facts while differing on their interpretation. There can be no doubt that the inflation was not stopped. But I should never have expected it to be stopped by the financial policies actually pursued. And this applies particularly to the effects of the changes in interest rates during this period, in regard to which, if I may say so with respect, the Committee seem to me to fail conspicuously to distinguish between money rates of interest and their real equivalent. For, surely, while prices were rising, as they were then, at rates up to 6 per cent per annum, the real rates represented by the money rates of the period were near zero or even negative. In such circumstances, what possible reason was there to expect borrowers to be deterred by small changes? The astonishing thing, I suggest, was not that these changes did not stop inflation, but that they should have had any influence at all. And if we reflect upon the general set of policy in those days, the make-up of the budget almost always working against monetary policy and a debt policy liable to offset any serious credit restriction, it is difficult not to agree with the Governor of the Bank of England when he described anything that he was able to do as mere 'spitting in the wind'.

v

I have now set forth my criticism both of the Committee's conception of the monetary mechanism and of their estimate of its potential effectiveness. At this point, despite all that I have said, I can imagine a would-be conciliator asking whether, after all, the differences disclosed are not really differences of degree rather than of kind.

So far as each particular point is concerned, save in regard to velocity of circulation and any implied passivity of money supply, I would not be unwilling to concede something to this attitude. Certainly, I would not claim any finality for my own arguments : one cannot ponder long over these matters without becoming acutely aware of the need for further analysis and empirical testing. Nevertheless, the differences are in the same direction all the time ; and although in most cases they may not amount to anything utterly fundamental, yet, cumulatively, I fancy that they do amount to a very considerable divergence.

This emerges very clearly if — by way of winding up — we glance for a moment at the implications for policy of the different analytical attitudes involved. Any apparent possibility of reconciliation under some general formula disappears completely as soon as we descend to detail.

Thus, the Committee lay great emphasis on the importance of debt management. One of the few concise statements among their conclusions is that 'debt management has become the fundamental domestic task of the central bank' (para. 982).

Now so long as this remains in general terms, I can subscribe to this — although, as a matter of drafting, I should have preferred 'of the government in relation to monetary policy' instead of 'of the central bank', for I cannot see how the unfortunate central bank is to manage the debt effectively if government policy is not favourable : and I cannot see governments allowing central banks to determine either the volume or the nature of their borrowings. But I do very much agree that in modern circumstances debt management is central to the working of the monetary mechanism; and I regard it as an element of lasting value in the Committee's report that it has emphasized this point.

But, as soon as we begin to spell out what debt management means, fundamental differences at once begin to emerge.

Thus, from my point of view, the major objective of debt management in relation to monetary policy should be the arrangement of short-term borrowing so as to harmonize with the aims of the central bank with regard to the credit base. At an earlier stage of this argument I have dealt with the deficiencies in this respect of the recent position in the United Kingdom, and when I talk of the desirability of debt management in connection with the working of the monetary mechanism, it is the rectification of these deficiencies that I have in mind.

But not so with the Committee. So far as funding short-term debt is concerned — the obvious method of restoring control of the money supply to the central bank — they are very Laodicean, on grounds which I personally find very unconvincing indeed.[1] And their major recommendations are of an entirely different nature. For the Committee, it is not the supply of money but the long-term rate, or structure of rates, which must be the focus of attention. In any given situation they suggest the authorities should take a view of what is the most appropriate long-term rate and then endeavour by explanation and appropriate action to keep actual rates at or near that level. They are against complete

---

[1] Namely, that some of the existing institutions of the money market might be embarrassed. But these institutions are not ends in themselves. And if restoration of control necessarily involves embarrassing them, then embarrassed they ought to be.

stabilization of rates. But they are also against frequent or energetic changes.

I confess that I find this extraordinarily difficult to swallow. From my point of view, once the control of money supply is assured, the focus of policy should not be the maintenance of some structure of rates which the authorities deem appropriate, but rather manipulations of supply such as to achieve, *via whatever movements of rates and credit rationing market conditions bring about,* the general aims and objectives of monetary policy — stable prices, high levels of activity, external equilibrium, in whatever combination is deemed to be appropriate. So far as the long-term rate is concerned, I certainly agree that government borrowing, especially for the nationalized industries, should be managed in harmony with these general aims. But I would say quite definitely that it is not the duty of a central bank to interfere with what movements of long-term rates its general operations on the credit base bring about. The objectives are in the field of general activity and it is on these — whatever they may be — rather than on movements of long-term rates that those responsible for monetary policy should concentrate their attention. In some circumstances, for instance, measures to stabilize the value of money may involve high long-term rates, in other circumstances, low ones. Having regard to the almost infinite complications of the influences working in the market, I suggest that the authorities are more likely to achieve their ultimate objectives if they keep their eye fixed on these goals and their hands on the controls of the credit base, than if they fuss themselves about divergences in the yield of long-term debt from some norm which they have decided to be appropriate.

For much the same reason, I would like to express the view that the correct conduct of policy, far from demanding fewer changes of interest rates as seems to be suggested by the Committee, in fact demands changes which will probably be more frequent and perhaps more vigorous than in the past. The Committee seem to think that changes of this sort must necessarily involve very grave danger to the existing institutions of the market.    On which I would comment, that if indeed existing institutions were indeed so fragile, it would be desirable to re-model them so as to eliminate such weakness.    But in fact I doubt the diagnosis.    We have all heard of one or two near things.    But the number of financial institutions ruined by the post-war fall in gilt-edged securities is not conspicuous — to put it mildly.    Personally, I should be very inclined to doubt whether, once we had got the inflation reasonably under control and expectations had adjusted themselves accordingly, the fluctuations in long-term rates which would be caused by monetary policy as I conceive it, would be very spectacular.    But this is a matter of conjecture.    What is necessary, I am convinced, are policies which are quick to adapt themselves to changing situations and are not inhibited by unnecessary conceptions of normality — which in this connection are either likely to be superfluous or out of date.


## VI

In conclusion, let me once more advert to the broad differences of underlying conceptions which divide the Committee from their critics.[1]

If the question is posed, what has been the main consideration determining the Committee's rejection of the interpretation of the monetary mechanism which begins from the control of the credit base, the answer, I conjecture, must be framed in terms of the weight of evidence which they received concerning the multiplication of credit agencies and credit facilities not directly within the immediate ambit of the Bank of England and the Clearing Banks.    They seem to have felt that fluctuations in the volume of spending, originating in this penumbra, were potentially so great as to demand a new approach to the analysis of aggregate demand — an approach in which the supply of money in the traditional theory played a very subsidiary part.    I get this impression strongly from the two very interesting articles

---

[1] This section was not read to the Seminar; it has been added since.

which Professor Sayers has published on this subject; [1] and re-reading the relevant portions of the Report in the light of his elucidations, this interpretation imposes itself again and again.

On this, what I have said already is an immanent critique. But to bring matters fully into the open, I will conclude with the following comments.

First, I am myself doubtful whether the developments are on such a scale as to transform the situation quite so radically as the Committee appear to suppose, nor do I believe that the influence and significance of the penumbra has been so neglected by traditional earlier thought on the subject as the attitude of the Committee might appear to suggest. I learnt a good deal of my analysis in this respect from Lavington's fine book on *The English Capital Market*: and although, needless to say, it is very out of date in much of its detailed description of the relevant institutions and policies, it certainly does not neglect this aspect of the general working of the system. There, right in the centre of the main theoretical discussion, in a chapter headed 'The Supply of Money: its technical efficiency',[2] we find the following observations:

> In addition to the various forms of currency manufactured by the specialized institutions of the market is the purchasing power created by manufacturers, merchants and others when they allow their customers to buy goods from them on an implicit promise to pay recorded in the form of a book debt. It may be objected that this system of trade credit does nothing but postpone payment, that it merely defers the use of currency and consequently adds nothing to the average volume of purchasing power. This would be only partially true if the total volume of book debts were always about the same; for although in that case the creation of new book debts would proceed concurrently with the extinction of old book debts by the use of currency, it would still be true that the average volume of purchasing power had been increased by the mere fact that payment was deferred. The average volume of these

[1] 'Monetary Thought and Monetary Policy in England', *Economic Journal*, December 1960, pp. 710-24 and 'Alternative Views of Central Banking', *Economica*, May 1961, pp. 111-24.   [2] *Op. cit.* pp. 39-40.

deferred payments would still constitute a net addition to the total stock of purchasing power, for corresponding to it would be an average volume of goods purchased without the use of currency. The significance of book debts, however, lies less in the addition which they make to the average volume of purchasing power than in the ease with which they are expanded and contracted, and in the fact that these variations are free from any control on the part of the market organizations whose business it is to regulate the supply of purchasing power. If, for example, the immediate outlook is favourable and business men wish to increase largely their stocks of materials and finished goods, their ability to purchase against book entries constitutes a net addition to the total volume of purchasing power in the same way as, in similar circumstances, would an expansion of cheque currency. But while the latter form of expansion is more obvious and can be dealt with by the Bank of England or the banks generally, the former kind of expansion is quite beyond their control.[1]

But — and this brings me to my second comment — neither Lavington nor the many other writers of the same tradition would have regarded this as an argument for denying the rôle of the supply of money in the usual sense of the term. On the contrary, they would have regarded it as an argument for using the power to vary that magnitude with greater strength and decision than otherwise would have been the case. Thus, reverting to this problem later on in his book, in the chapter on the 'Regulation of the Currency', Lavington urges that 'at such times when the purchasing

---

[1] It should not be thought that this is the first passage of this sort in the literature. The tradition goes back a long way. In Hume's essay on *Public Credit*, it is argued that 'Public securities are with us, become a kind of money, and pass as readily at the current price as gold or silver. Whenever any profitable undertaking offers itself, . . . there are never wanting hands enow to embrace it : nor need a trader, who has sums in the public stocks, fear to launch out into the most extensive trade ; since he is possessed of funds, which will answer the most sudden demand that can be made upon him. No merchant thinks it necessary to keep by him any considerable cash. Bank stocks, or India-bonds, especially the latter, serve all the same purposes, because he can dispose of them, or pledge them to a banker, in a quarter of an hour. . . . In short, our national debts furnish merchants with a species of money that is continually multiplying in their hands. . . .' *Essays*, Ed. Greene and Grose, vol. i, p. 363.

power of the community has already been increased by action on the part of the public and rising confidence has been reinforced by rising prices, it seems probable that the true loan policy of the Banks lies not in an expansion of their loans but rather in *a contraction designed to counteract the effects of increased purchasing power* [1] . . .' (my italics).

My own view entirely coincides with this. I find it extremely difficult to suppose that, even to-day, the elasticity of trade credit is such as to be able more than to counterbalance practicable contractions of the credit base and their consequential influence on interest rates. The belief that it would be so, only seems to me to begin to become plausible if one ignores, as the Committee seems to ignore, the fundamental difference between monetary and non-monetary liquidity, on which I have expatiated above. Admittedly, when the process of contraction or deceleration begins, there may be enough potential slack in the trade credit sector to offset it. But it would seem to me to be highly unlikely that this offset would not fairly soon encounter increasing resistance. The occasions on which trade credit has increased in the past in the face of credit contraction and money interest rates high enough to offset anticipations of price rises, are surely very few.[2] Indeed, I have yet to

---

[1] *Ibid.* p. 173.

[2] In this connection, there is a sentence in Professor Sayers' address to the British Association which seems to call for comment. Referring to policies which proceed *via* control of money supply, he says, 'It follows that a policy of *stablizing* [my italics] bank deposits and waiting for the expanding volume of payments to force interest rates upward . . . is not enough: action would be always too late, as it was when strain on the note issue was expected to set the corrective mechanism in motion'. (*Economic Journal*, vol. lxx, p. 724.) I do not disagree with this so far as it goes. But I would disagree very strongly if it were thought to dispose of the policy of operating *via* the money supply. For why should it be suggested that the limit of operations of this sort is a *stabilization* of deposits? What is clearly needed is operations by the central bank which prevent an undue increase in the aggregate volume of spending; and if this involves a positive contraction of the credit base, it will be failing in its duty if it does not bring it about. I ought to add that, just after the sentence I have quoted, Professor Sayers goes on to say that the only remedy on the monetary side is a policy of interest rates much more vigorous than has been tried hitherto. If this is a positive recommendation, and not just an indication of how hopeless the situation is, there is surely scope here for very considerable *rapprochement*. We can leave to the academic grove further talk

read a convincing account of one. Certainly the results of the attempts made before 1957 by our own authorities are no example of such a breakdown.

But let us suppose that the situation is more serious than this; that the spread of financial institutions with power to stoke up trade credit to a much greater degree than ever before is making the task of the central bank, if not impossible, at least a matter of appalling difficulty — especially from the point of view of public relations. What then? Surely *to invent methods of bringing these institutions within range of the central bank discipline.* That was the way Mr. Riefler reacted, when he was pressed: if institutions outside the Reserve system were to develop credit creating powers of an embarrassing nature, then they would have to be regulated (Evidence Q. 9830-51). That was his point of view. Then why should we not be prepared to do likewise? Why do we assume that human ingenuity is exhausted in this respect — at any rate on this side of the Atlantic? Why should we more or less abandon belief in the whole apparatus of monetary control and sadly pin all our hopes of stabilizing a free system on fiscal methods whose efficacy in practice up to date has certainly been no better than that of old-fashioned monetary policy carried out with determination? It really should not be beyond the wit of man to maintain control over the effective supply of money; and, as I conceive matters, eventually little less than the future of free societies may very well depend on our doing so.

about the priority of variations in rates of interest and the supply of money, and address ourselves to persuading the government and the bank of the desirability of a strong monetary policy; and if Professor Sayers has inhibitions about stressing the supply of money, I shall not cavil at this point, knowing that to get his effective interest rates, he certainly will have to operate on that factor. But I am bound to say that I get no such impression from the Report itself.

# SELECT INDEX OF NAMES

227

Moore, Mr. Henry: his debt to tradition, 60

Paish, Professor Frank: his proposal of emergency revival of the system of Treasury deposit receipts, 184; his proposal for a general sales tax with exemption allowances, 187
Pareto: his pretence of an Olympian detachment, 7
Paul III: his alleged defence of Cellini's misdeeds, 75
Perroux, Professor François, 3
Physiocrats: their failure to distinguish between positive and normative judgments transcended by subsequent thought, 19; cited by Hayek as entertaining 'false' theories of individualism, 95
Picasso: his debt to tradition, 60
Pigou: his propositions on the economics of welfare not independent of underlying political assumptions, 14, 15
Plato: his economic generalizations intimately concerned with conceptions of political obligation, 5; his *Republic* an example of the valuation of social relationships in terms of the intrinsic excellence of certain patterns, 30; his willingness to destroy the family, 77
Popper, Professor Karl: his analysis of Plato's social philosophy cited, 30; on the fallacy of holism, 96

Quesnay: his economic generalizations part of an exposition of natural law, 5; his picture of a system of harmonious economic relations, 9

Radcliffe Committee on the Working of the Monetary Mechanism: critical discussion of its report, 197-226
Raphael: the dependence of his work on demand from public patrons, 55
Renoir: the high valuation of his works in recent market transactions, 65
Ricardo: his awareness of the extra-economic, 6; significance of the conjunction of his theory of the distribution of the precious metals

and the theory of comparative costs, 141
Riefler, Mr. W.: his insistence on the key importance of the credit base, 199; on the necessity of controlling all credit creating institutions, 226
Robertson, Sir Dennis: denies usefulness of complete assimilation of bank deposits to other forms of liquidity, 205
Robinson, F. J. (Viscount Godrich): his splendid justification for the foundation of the National Gallery, 61-2
Rousseau: cited by Hayek as entertaining false theories of individualism, 95
Royal Commission on Taxation of Profits and Income: its somewhat surprising support of the tax on marriage, 88-90
Rubens: the high valuation of his works in recent market transactions, 65

Samuelson, Professor Paul: his articles on public expenditure cited, 18
Sayers, Professor R. S.: his important demonstration of the significance of the floating debt for monetary policy, 175-201; his presidential address to the British Association cited, 197, 223; suggests that bank deposits may come to be regarded as small change of the monetary system, 200; compares differences of opinion regarding the theory of the Radcliffe Committee with differences of opinion between the Banking and Currency Schools, 204, 208
Senior: on the distinction between political economy as an art and as a science, 6; his conception of a separation between considerations appropriate to the pursuit of wealth and other objectives, 13
Shaw, Bernard: his support of strict equality of income, 78
Shelley: his *Prometheus Unbound* recommended as representative of the positive aspirations of liberalism, 135; his sympathy with Italian and Greek nationalism, 145

# SELECT INDEX OF NAMES

Sidgwick: his distinction between normative and positive propositions in social studies, 6; his classification by Hayek among 'false' individualists, 99

Simons, Henry: his recommendation of rules rather than authorities, 48

Sinclair, Sir John: his list of unfulfilled predictions of economic catastrophe, 111

Smith, Adam: on the object of political economy, 5-6; his picture of a system of harmonious economic relations, 9; his failure to distinguish between positive and normative judgments transcended by subsequent thought, 19; limitations of his theory of the market in relation to aggregate stability, 43, 44; his recognition of the way in which intervention by one state may compel intervention by others, 49; his belief in the absence of congenital differences, 75; cited by Hayek as exponent of 'true' individualism, 95; provides some justification for progressive taxation, 105; his demonstration of the benefits of the industrial division of labour, 141; his vision of an empire embracing both the American colonies and the United Kingdom, 152

Spencer, Herbert: a typical representative of the extreme *laissez-faire* tradition, 41, 42; his doctrinaire individualism compared to the attitude of Bentham, 106

Stalin, Joseph: the highly deleterious effect of his policies on the visual arts and music, 57

Stephen, Fitzjames: his attack on Mill's conception of liberty, 31-3

Steuart, Sir James: his attack on the quantity theory of money, 209

Titian: the dependence of his work on demand from public patrons,

55; the protests against the purchase of his *Vendramin Family* before the First World War no longer typical of the attitude of the general public, 69

Tocqueville: his immunity from *bourgeois* interest, 8

Torrens, Robert: his recommendation of compensation funds to promote mobility, 51; his suggestion of an imperial *Zollverein*, 131; the inventor of the term 'territorial division of labour', 141; his terms of trade argument against unilateral free trade, 143

Utilitarians, the nineteenth-century: cited by Hayek as entertaining 'false' theories of individualism, 95

Van Eyck: the high valuation of his works in recent market transactions, 65

Verwoerd, Dr.: his obvious disbelief in the principle of equality before law, 74

Viner, Professor Jacob: his distinction between trade creating and trade diverting effects of customs unions, 116

Voltaire: on Russian laws in relation to immigration, 121

Waverley: Committee on the Export of Works of Art, 69

Wicksell: his discussion of the benefit principle of taxation, 17; denial of the relevance of his famous model with only one rate of interest to judgment under current conditions of the relative importance of interest rates or the supply of money, 210

Wiseman, J.: his views on the finance of education cited, 108

Young, Arthur: his critique of Sir James Steuart's attack on the quantity theory, 209